OCCASIONAL PAPER **82**

Characteristics of a Successful Exchange Rate System

Jacob A. Frenkel, Morris Goldstein, and Paul R. Masson

INTERNATIONAL MONETARY FUND
Washington DC
July 1991

Library of Congress Cataloging-in-Publication Data

Frenkel, Jacob A.
    Characteristics of a successful exchange rate system / by Jacob A.
Frenkel, Morris Goldstein, and Paul R. Masson.
      p. cm. — (Occasional paper / International Monetary Fund,
ISSN 0251-6365 ; 82)
    Includes bibliographical references.
    ISBN 1-55775-215-X
    1. Foreign exchange problem. 2. Monetary policy. I. Goldstein,
Morris, 1944– . II. Masson, Paul R., 1946– . III. Title.
IV. Series: Occasional paper (International Monetary Fund) : no. 82.
HG3851.F69 1991
332.4'5—dc20   91-21414
                                                         CIP

Price: US$10.00
(US$7.50 to full-time faculty members and
students at universities and colleges)

Please send orders to:
International Monetary Fund, Publication Services
700 19th Street, N.W., Washington, D.C. 20431, U.S.A.
Tel.: (202) 623-7430   Telefax: (202) 623-7201

Contents

Charts

The following symbols have been used throughout this paper:

...   to indicate that data are not available;

—   to indicate that the figure is zero or less than half the final digit shown, or that the item does not exist;

–   between years or months (e.g., 1990–91 or January–June) to indicate the years or months covered, including the beginning and ending years or months;

/   between years (e.g., 1990/91) to indicate a crop or fiscal (financial) year.

"Billion" means a thousand million.

Minor discrepancies between constituent figures and totals are due to rounding.

The term "country," as used in this paper, does not in all cases refer to a territorial entity that is a state as understood by international law and practice; the term also covers some territorial entities that are not states, but for which statistical data are maintained and provided internationally on a separate and independent basis.

Preface

This study, which was prepared in the Research Department of the International Monetary Fund, addresses a number of issues that relate to the operation of the international monetary system. It extends the analysis in several earlier studies by the authors (see the list of references). The study is designed to be accessible to the nonspecialist; however, some technical issues are treated in the appendices.

The authors are Jacob A. Frenkel, Economic Counselor and Director of Research; Morris Goldstein, Deputy Director of the Research Department; and Paul R. Masson, Advisor. They are especially grateful to Claire Adams for research assistance, to the editor Elin Knotter of the External Relations Department, and to Andrea Chisholm for her efficient word processing. Numerous colleagues provided comments and advice. The authors alone are responsible for the study; the opinions expressed are theirs and do not necessarily reflect the views of the IMF.

I Introduction

The purpose of this paper is to identify key characteristics of a successful exchange rate system. To keep the paper manageable, two restrictions have been placed on its scope. First, although some issues raised have wider applicability, the discussion concentrates on industrial countries. A separate Occasional Paper discusses exchange rate policies for developing countries.[1] Second, the implications of international capital flows for the exchange rate system are not discussed here and are treated in another Occasional Paper.[2]

This paper focuses on the interaction between macroeconomic policy—particularly monetary policy—and the degree of exchange rate flexibility in industrial countries.[3] Much of the discussion revolves around the issues of if and how the international monetary system can be designed to reconcile the objectives of price stability and exchange market stability—and in the face of different country circumstances. Exchange rate commitments should certainly not deflect monetary policy from its prime objective of pursuing price stability. At the same time, where the credibility of anti-inflationary policy is not strong, exchange rate commitments may assist in achieving the objective of price stability. The paper also considers more generally the coordination of economic policies, which is necessary for the smooth operation of any exchange rate system.

Section II discusses how nominal anchors for the international monetary system might be established so as to prevent a tendency to systemic inflation or deflation. Section III addresses the issues of how the international monetary system can facilitate international adjustment; it draws the distinction between ''desirable'' and ''undesirable'' current account imbalances and suggests how undesirable imbalances should be corrected. Section IV examines criteria that might be helpful in deciding how countries with different characteristics might choose the most appropriate exchange rate policy. Section V introduces the implications of exchange market stability having a ''public goods'' character for the systemic responsibilities of the largest industrial countries. Section VI discusses the need for international policy coordination and some obstacles to its implementation, whereas some technical aspects of such coordination are treated in Appendices I and II. Section VII deals with the role of the IMF in the evolving international monetary system, including its role with respect to the SDR.

---

[1] Aghevli, Khan, and Montiel (1991).

[2] Goldstein and others (1991).

[3] The analysis draws on some of the discussion in Frenkel, Goldstein, and Masson (1988, 1989a, 1989b, and 1991).

II Nominal Anchors

Any successful exchange rate system needs some mechanism for avoiding both global inflation and deflation. Clearly, exchange rates alone cannot serve as the nominal anchor for the system. Not all countries can simultaneously rely on fixed nominal exchange rates to guide their monetary policies aimed at achieving price stability. At least one country has to set the inflation rate for the system as a whole.

Two crucial questions arise in this context. First, if the responsibility for establishing the nominal anchor falls to the largest industrial countries—as we think it should—what degree of symmetry should exist among them in sharing this responsibility? Second, does the maintenance of a nominal anchor require something beyond the commitments of domestic monetary authorities to price stability with sustainable growth?

In considering the question of symmetry, it should be recalled that the relative importance of the largest industrial countries in world economic activity and finance has become more equal since the 1950s and 1960s, the heyday of the Bretton Woods system (Table 1). The share of the United States in output has declined substantially, as has the dollar's share in official reserves—primarily vis-à-vis Japan and Germany. The U.S. share of world trade has declined only slightly, but Japanese and German shares have expanded markedly relative to other countries. As a result of these changes, it is unrealistic to expect a return to a system in which the United States provides the sole nominal anchor.[4]

In the absence of a single dominant country, it is natural to consider price stability as the *collective* responsibility of the largest industrial countries. After all, the monetary policies of the three largest industrial countries—the United States, Japan, and Germany—have the largest impact on world output and inflation. Moreover, none of the three is likely (other than in most unusual circumstances) to subordinate monetary policy to the exchange rate when the latter would require a policy that conflicted with domestic

Table 1. Shares of Selected Countries in World Totals
(In percent)

	United States	Japan	Germany	Other
Share of national currencies in total identified official reserve holdings[1]				
1968	80.0	—	1.5	18.5
1975	85.1	0.6	6.6	7.7
1989	60.2	7.9	19.3	12.6
Share of world trade[2]				
1956	16.2	3.3	7.4	73.1
1980	12.6	7.1	9.9	70.5
1989	14.6	8.2	10.4	66.8
Share of world output[3]				
1962	30.4	6.2	9.1	54.3
1980	25.4	10.2	8.0	56.4
1988	25.3	11.2	7.3	56.2

[1] International Monetary Fund, *Annual Report*, 1975, 1980, and 1990. Data for 1968 are official claims on the United States or Germany, divided by total identified claims; data for Japan were not reported, and are assumed to be zero. Official Eurodollar holdings were added to the U.S. figures.
[2] Based on the sum of imports plus exports. *International Financial Statistics, Supplement on Trade Statistics*, Supplement Series, No. 15, 1988; *International Financial Statistics, Yearbook, 1990.*
[3] Real GDP at market prices. *International Financial Statistics, Supplement on Output Statistics*, Supplement Series, No. 8, 1984, and *International Financial Statistics, Yearbook, 1990.* Calculated using 1980 GDP at current market prices (in U.S. dollars) and real GDP growth rates.

objectives.[5] Such a conflict can arise, for example, when a country faces both excess demand conditions and upward pressure on its exchange rate; in such

---

[4]Until 1968, the United States undertook the commitment to exchange U.S. dollars for gold at a fixed price.

[5]Some recent public statements by central bank officials in these three countries are instructive.

Vice-President Schlesinger of the Deutsche Bundesbank has argued:

circumstances, lowering domestic interest rates to prevent the exchange rate from rising (appreciating) above its target would add to inflationary pressures.

The inflation record since 1950, taken as a whole, suggests that the United States, Japan, and Germany have been more successful in limiting increases in prices

"... nor can it in the future become the central banks' main function, regardless of the prevailing circumstances, to try to implement fixed targets for exchange rate movements . . . . Central banks' most important function . . . resides in the fact that they collectively bear the ultimate responsibility for the 'global rate of inflation' and that each individual major central bank is responsible for the stability of the purchasing power of its own currency.'' (1988, p. 32)

Former Executive Director Suzuki of the Bank of Japan has put forth a similar view:

"In the three major currency areas, therefore, monetary policy priority should basically be assigned to maintaining stable domestic prices.'' (1989, p. 6)

The overriding concern for domestic price stability has also been reiterated recently by Chairman Greenspan of the U.S. Federal Reserve System:

"The current [zero-inflation] resolution is laudable, in part because it directs monetary policy toward a single goal, price stability, that monetary policy is uniquely suited to pursue.'' (1990, p. 5)

than the average of the other Group of Ten countries (Table 2). Central banks in each of the three countries have a substantial measure of independence, though more so in the United States and Germany than in Japan.[6] Central bank independence and past success in achieving low rates of inflation help reinforce the policy credibility of central banks. It is also important that a consensus exists in each of the three countries to resist threats to price stability. Given their dominant size in the world economy, and their ability to commit monetary policies credibly to achieving price stability, the three countries can be seen as the nucleus of a "low-inflation club" that, in concert with other countries, can seek to prevent global inflation or deflation.[7]

Some have suggested, however, that establishing a

[6]Fiscal policy can assist in establishing a nominal anchor by forgoing excessive debt accumulation that itself handicaps the ability of the monetary authorities to carry out their task.

[7]Failure to maintain good inflation performance would be expected to lead, inter alia, to a decline in the reserve currency role of a large country.

Table 2. Inflation Performance of Selected Industrial Countries
(Annual averages, in percent)

	1954–89	1954–60	1961–70	1971–80	1981–89
Average of rate of change of consumer prices					
United States	4.4	1.5	2.8	7.8	4.7
Japan	5.0	1.9	5.8	9.1	2.0
Germany	3.1	1.6	2.6	5.1	2.6
Other G-10[1]	6.1	2.6	3.8	10.5	6.7
Standard deviation of rate of change of consumer prices					
United States	3.3	1.2	1.7	3.1	2.3
Japan	4.4	2.5	1.3	5.4	1.4
Germany	1.8	0.7	0.7	1.3	2.0
Other G-10[1]	3.8	1.5	0.8	3.0	3.1
Average of rate of change of GDP/GNP deflators					
United States	4.5	2.6	3.1	7.4	4.4
Japan	4.7	3.5	5.5	7.7	1.3
Germany	3.7	2.4	3.7	5.3	2.8
Other G-10[1]	6.4	2.8	4.2	10.9	6.6
Standard deviation of rate of change of GDP/GNP deflators					
United States	2.5	0.8	1.6	1.6	2.1
Japan	3.9	2.6	1.3	5.0	0.9
Germany	1.8	1.4	1.6	1.4	0.9
Other G-10[1]	3.7	1.6	0.9	2.6	2.7

Source: International Monetary Fund, *International Financial Statistics*.
[1] Weighted by three-year centered moving averages of GNP. Other Group of Ten countries are France, Italy, the United Kingdom, Canada, Sweden, the Netherlands, Belgium, and Switzerland.

nominal anchor will require something more than a commitment to monetary stability by the major countries. Are there international monetary rules of some kind, including external pegs (for example, to gold or to a commodity basket) or targets for world intermediate variables (for example, a world monetary aggregate or nominal income), that are likely to enhance global inflation performance and as a result contribute to the successful operation of the international monetary system? There is extensive literature on the merits of rules versus discretion in the domestic policy arena, and many of the arguments are also relevant to the international monetary system.[8] In principle, a rule for anchoring the price level should focus expectations, discipline policies, and reduce price level uncertainty. It should also help to reduce negotiating costs and other costs that would be associated with a more discretionary system. However, rule-based systems often turn out to be less automatic in practice than in theory.[9] Rules impart

discipline to macroeconomic policies only if penalties for breaking the rules are significant. Though rules may reduce the uncertainty inherent in discretionary policies, they may also impart a lack of flexibility to the system, which prevents adequate response to unforeseen circumstances.[10]

On a broader level, the evidence suggests that explicit international anchoring rules have not consistently yielded better inflation performance. Cooper (1982), for example, documents large, long-run swings in wholesale prices—of about 30–70 percent in both directions—during the nineteenth century gold standard. In addition, Meltzer (1986) found that short-term prediction errors for prices were much higher during the gold standard (1890–1914) than during the 1950–80 period (Table 3). Similarly, one would not expect stability of consumer prices to follow from stability of commodity prices; there have been extended periods during which the two sets of prices moved in divergent directions.[11]

---

[8]See Frenkel, Goldstein, and Masson (1988), pp. 160–62.

[9]For instance, the specie-flow mechanism of the pre-World War I gold standard was often undermined by the sterilization operations of domestic monetary authorities.

[10]For instance, the usefulness of domestic monetary targets has been greatly hampered by shifts in the public's demand for money associated with financial innovations.

[11]Boughton and Branson (1988).

Table 3. Variance of the Forecast Error of Log Levels of Selected U.S. Macroeconomic Variables

	Nominal GNP	Price Level	Real GNP	Money M1	M2
1890 (I)–1914 (IV)	0.298	0.025	0.283	—	0.026
1915 (I)–1931 (III)	0.180	0.060	0.141	0.026	0.020
1931 (IV)–1941 (IV)	0.564	0.024	0.402	0.043	0.163
1942 (I)–1951 (I)	0.067	0.060	0.078	0.031	0.020
1951 (II)–1971 (III)	0.013	0.002	0.011	0.005	0.003
1971 (IV)–1980 (IV)	0.013	0.002	0.014	0.009	0.004

Source: Meltzer (1986), Table 4-3. The forecasts were generated using a multistate Kalman filter, with coefficients updated each period.

III Facilitating International Adjustment

Even if price stability is—and should be—the primary focus of monetary policies in the largest industrial countries, a successful international monetary system cannot ignore the international repercussions of domestic monetary and fiscal policies.

In the present context of high capital mobility, large external current account imbalances and real exchange rate misalignments can develop. Table 4 indicates that current account imbalances were larger, on average, in the 1980s than in earlier decades, and Chart 1 shows that fluctuations of both nominal and real effective exchange rates have been large. The issue then arises of whether domestic monetary and fiscal policies should be adjusted to offset—at least partially—external disequilibria.

If the international monetary system is to succeed in withstanding a variety of shocks and in preventing undesirable and unsustainable accumulation of foreign assets and liabilities, it should embody mechanisms that identify and resist certain large current account positions, but not others. Current account imbalances arise from a variety of sources, some of which are benign and require no policy intervention, and some of which are undesirable and do require intervention. Benign imbalances, for example, could include current account surpluses or deficits that are related either to private sector saving patterns which reflect different demographic developments,[12] or to different investment opportunities. Other examples are the consumption-smoothing of a temporary terms of trade shock, or the current account fluctuations owing to different relative cyclical positions.[13]

Undesirable current account imbalances include those that reflect distortions in the economy and those that involve persistent and unsustainable accumulation of foreign assets or liabilities. The latter can lead to subsequent disruption in financial markets and to sharp changes in consumption and investment when they are reversed. What constitutes an undesirable or unsustain-

---

[12] See *World Economic Outlook*, October 1989, Chapter II.

[13] In practice, identification of a "temporary" terms of trade shock may be difficult in situations like the prolonged slump of commodity prices in the 1980s and the prolonged boom of oil prices in much of the 1970s.

Table 4. Three Major Industrial Countries: Balances of Payments on Current Account
(As a percent of GDP)

	1960–64	1965–69	1970–74	1975–79	1980–84	1985–89
			Annual averages			
United States	0.7	0.3	0.1	—	− 0.7	− 3.0
Japan	− 0.6	0.8	0.9	0.6	0.9	3.3
Germany	0.8	1.1	1.2	0.7	0.2	4.0
			Persistence[1]			
United States	—	0.9	− 0.3	0.3	2.0	0.5
Japan	—	− 0.3	0.5	0.1	1.1	0.6
Germany	—	0.5	0.5	—	0.9	0.5

Source: International Monetary Fund, *World Economic Outlook*.
[1] As measured by the first-order serial-correlation coefficient for the current account ratio. Insufficient data were available for the first subperiod, since a lagged value is needed for the calculation.

Chart 1. Quarterly Average Nominal and Real Effective Exchange Rates, First Quarter 1960–Fourth Quarter 1990
(Indices, 1980 =100; logarithmic scale)

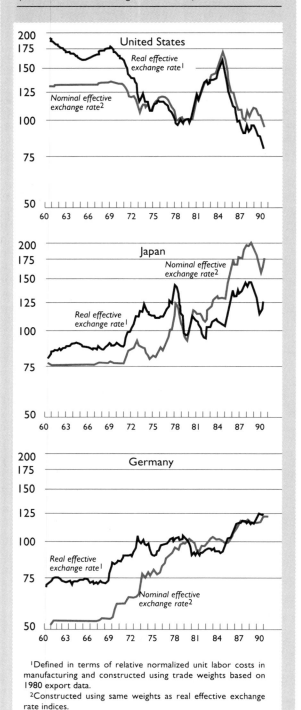

[1]Defined in terms of relative normalized unit labor costs in manufacturing and constructed using trade weights based on 1980 export data.

[2]Constructed using same weights as real effective exchange rate indices.

able position—particularly under conditions of high capital mobility—is often subject to complex interpretation, however, and no simple criteria are available.

One type of concern derives from an undesirable and unsustainable fiscal deficit. The government fiscal position cannot, however, be the only criterion for judging whether the current account balance is appropriate, nor can the private sector's balance necessarily be declared healthy. First, the dividing line between private and public is not always easily made. For instance, the government may eventually have to shoulder financial losses caused by what are in the first instance private sector decisions (for example, the bailout of U.S. Savings and Loans). Second, tax rates and government regulations affect private incentives to save and invest, and hence it cannot be assumed that private sector decisions are undistorted. Third, rates of return to saving and investment may be affected by market failures of various sorts, such as speculative bubbles in financial markets. Fourth, private decisions may not adequately incorporate effects on social welfare, because there are external effects on other domestic or foreign residents or because too little account is taken of the interests of future generations.

It is also not true that investment is always to be favored over consumption, and hence that current account deficits are benign if they involve increases in the former but not the latter. For new investment to be desirable, the social rate of return on that investment—including both the private return and increases in tax revenue accruing to the host country—should exceed the cost of borrowing. Clearly, the indiscriminate lending during the 1970s to developing countries for investment projects that were not economically viable was not in the best interests of the world economy (or of the national economies concerned). On the other hand, a current account deficit associated with a decline in private saving in response to a temporary decline in exports would be appropriate if it prevented a sharp fall in domestic consumption.

An evaluation of the desirability and sustainability of current account positions raises at least three questions. First, is the fiscal position appropriate, in the sense that expenditures reflect social needs, and financing incorporates tax smoothing and burden sharing across generations? Second, if current account deficits correspond to increased investment, is the rate of return on that investment greater than the cost of borrowing, from the point of view of society as a whole? Here, the relevant rate of return should be the before-tax return (assuming that the income is taxed where it is earned), since the country benefits from increased tax revenue even if the private investor does not.[14] Third, if current

---

[14]Conversely, investment that is induced by tax incentives may not pay a sufficient return to benefit society as a whole, even if the return to the private investor exceeds his borrowing cost.

account deficits correspond to increased consumption, is it temporary, and does it correspond to optimal consumption-smoothing in an intertemporal context? If the increase in consumption is likely to be more persistent, does it result from economic distortions?

In assessing whether current account imbalances are benign or malignant for a country individually, it must also be kept in mind that global consistency implies that current account positions are interdependent. Therefore, adjustment of one country's position will require other countries' positions to change—whether or not they are judged satisfactory from a domestic point of view. This interdependence also raises the danger that countries may aim to achieve current account positions that are globally inconsistent, and as a result policies impart an expansionary or contractionary bias to the world economy.[15] Some degree of international policy coordination is needed if current account objectives are an important element in policy setting (see Section VI below).

Table 5 illustrates changes in current account imbalances for a number of industrial countries during 1981–89. Using the familiar saving-investment identity for an open economy, current account positions are broken down into the government fiscal position, private saving, and private investment.[16] As is evident from the table, there is considerable diversity across countries in the origins of current account imbalances. In some cases (for example, the United States) a move to a current account deficit over this period was associated with an increased fiscal deficit, while in others (for example, the United Kingdom) the current account deteriorated despite a strengthening of the fiscal position. In some other countries (for example, Australia), a weakening of the current account reflected declines in private saving and investment, with the former falling more sharply. The countries with a current account surplus (in 1989) also display marked differences: whereas both Japan and Germany displayed improvements in the government's fiscal position, Japan showed an increase in private investment, and Germany a decline.

The data do not provide a clear message on whether the imbalances are cause for concern; a more in-depth analysis is required. They do suggest, however, that current account positions arise from a number of sources, and that it is necessary to know the source of the current account imbalance before a decision can be made on whether it needs correcting and how to correct it. The appropriate policy action is likely to be one that acts directly on private saving or investment, or on the government's fiscal position. For example, if the current

---

[15]Inconsistency of balance of payments targets in the Bretton Woods system is discussed in Hamada (1974).

[16]Each of these imbalances is affected by a number of variables, including real exchange rates and real interest rates.

Table 5. Selected Industrial Countries: Current Account Positions and Saving-Investment Imbalances, 1981–89[1]
(As percent of GNP)

	1981				1989				Change, 1981–89			
	CA	FP	PI	PS	CA	FP	PI	PS	CA	FP	PI	PS
United States	0.2	−1.0	16.1	17.3	−2.1	−2.0	14.4	14.2	−2.3	−1.0	−1.7	−3.1
Japan	0.4	−3.8	21.3	25.5	2.0	2.7	25.4	24.7	1.6	6.5	4.1	−0.8
Germany	−0.5	−3.7	18.5	21.6	4.6	0.2	17.9	22.4	5.2	3.9	−0.5	0.8
France	−0.9	−1.9	19.0	20.0	−0.4	−1.4	17.6	18.6	0.5	0.5	−1.5	−1.4
Italy	−2.3	−11.6	21.4	30.7	−1.2	−10.2	16.0	25.0	1.0	1.4	−5.4	−5.8
United Kingdom	2.6	−2.6	11.8	17.0	−3.7	1.3	16.6	11.6	−6.3	3.9	4.9	−5.4
Canada	−1.7	−1.5	21.5	21.3	−2.6	−3.4	19.7	20.5	−0.8	−1.9	−1.9	−0.8
Australia	−4.9	−1.2	19.1	15.4	−5.9	1.2	20.0	12.9	−1.0	2.4	0.8	−2.6
Belgium	−4.3	−13.1	13.6	22.4	2.4	−6.5	16.8	25.7	6.7	6.6	3.2	3.4
Denmark	−3.2	−6.9	12.5	16.2	−1.3	−0.4	15.5	14.6	1.9	6.5	3.0	−1.6
Netherlands	2.1	−5.5	16.0	23.6	3.3	−5.1	19.5	27.9	1.2	0.4	3.5	4.3
Norway	3.8	4.7	22.1	21.2	0.3	1.0	23.5	22.8	−3.5	−3.7	1.4	1.6
Spain	−2.8	−3.9	19.3	20.4	−2.9	−2.1	20.9	20.1	−0.1	1.8	1.6	−0.3

Source: International Monetary Fund, World Economic Outlook; Organization for Economic Cooperation and Development, Economic Outlook, and National Accounts, 1976–1988, Volume II.

[1] Variables are as follows: CA = current account position, FP = general government fiscal position, PI = private fixed investment, PS = private saving, calculated residually as CA + PI − FP.

account imbalance reflects a tax-induced distortion of private saving, the first-best policy would be to correct that distortion at its source (that is, by removing the tax distortion).

A similar judgment should be made about exchange rate fluctuations. If volatility is related to erratic shifts in asset preferences or speculative bubbles, exchange market intervention and adjustments in monetary policy can serve a very useful role. If exchange rate movements reflect fundamental factors affecting the relative attractiveness of different currencies, those exchange rate movements should not be resisted. Even if it is clear that a currency is "misaligned,"[17] the source of the misalignment is relevant: if overvaluation is due, for instance, to expansionary fiscal policy, resisting the overvaluation through expansionary monetary policy would compound the problem.[18]

---

[17]Williamson and Miller (1987) speak of misalignment when a currency deviates from its "fundamental equilibrium real exchange rate."

[18]Feldstein (1988).

IV Diversity in Exchange Arrangements

Since the breakdown of the Bretton Woods system, the exchange rate system has evolved in two distinct directions:[19] on the one side, there has been a move toward regional blocs of exchange rate stability—principally in Europe—but also including developing countries with fixed exchange rates vis-à-vis the U.S. dollar or the French franc, and with pegs to baskets of currencies; on the other, there has been greater flexibility between the major currencies.[20] As discussed below, there are good reasons why countries choose different exchange arrangements.

At least three factors seem to play a leading role in decisions on exchange arrangements. The first relates to *structural characteristics* of the economy, such as degree of openness, exposure to terms of trade shocks, and degree of nominal wage-price flexibility. A second important consideration is the *need to reinforce monetary policy credibility*; in some circumstances, this credibility can best be achieved through pegging to a "hard currency." A third criterion is the existence of *other commitments to regional integration*, which can reinforce—and be supported by—exchange rate commitments. Of course, the choices of countries to have more or less exchange rate flexibility are not independent: for example, if exchange rates between some key currencies are flexible, other countries have to accept a degree of exchange rate variability against one or another of these key currencies.

Structural Characteristics of Economies

One can imagine a continuum, starting from exchange rate flexibility at one end and going to complete fixity at the other. Exchange rate stability is desirable in itself because it is associated ceteris paribus with reduced uncertainty—but it may involve a loss of monetary autonomy that would be useful in adjusting to external or internal shocks. Structural characteristics of economies—familiar from the literature on optimal currency areas—influence the desirability of being at one or another point on that continuum. Fixed exchange rates are likely to be more desirable the more open the economy is, in the sense of being subjected to external *nominal* shocks, and the more integrated it is with its neighbors. Fixed nominal exchange rates require that adjustment to real shocks take place solely through changes in price and wage levels, or through factor mobility—whereas under flexible exchange rates, some of the adjustment can occur through nominal appreciation or depreciation. Therefore, flexibility in nominal magnitudes is especially important under fixed rates for minimizing the costs of real macroeconomic disturbances.[21] Groupings of countries or regions within which factors are free to move (such as states or provinces within a single country) are less likely to suffer from lack of flexibility of nominal exchange rates. Fiscal transfers, such as within a regional grouping like the European Community (EC), also help to alleviate costs of adjustment.

On the other hand, economies that are large producers of primary commodities, that is, resource-based economies, are more likely to face large external real shocks, resulting from large changes in the relative price of commodities vis-à-vis manufactures. Countries like Australia, New Zealand, and, to a lesser extent, Canada, have substantial exports of primary commodities, and face greater variability in their terms of trade than do other industrial countries. The experience of Australia and New Zealand is instructive. Until the early 1980s, both countries operated pegged exchange rates, the bilateral rate against the U.S. dollar in the case of Australia and an effective exchange rate in the case of New Zealand. Positive terms of trade shocks

---

[19]In addition to these developments in exchange arrangements, significant economic policy coordination has also emerged among the major industrial countries in the post-1985 period.

[20]As of March 31, 1990, 30 countries were classified as having currencies pegged to the U.S. dollar, 14 to the French franc, and 46 to other currencies or baskets of currencies; 13 currencies had limited flexibility vis-à-vis either a single currency or group of currencies; and 48 countries had "more flexible" exchange arrangements (International Monetary Fund (1990), Appendix Table II.17).

[21]The degree of nominal flexibility may itself depend on the monetary policy regime: a commitment to resist inflationary pressures may make labor and product markets more flexible, and thereby lower the unemployment costs of negative supply shocks. If a "hard currency" policy associated with a pegged exchange rate enhances the anti-inflationary commitment, it may also increase the economy's flexibility.

in the 1970s led to accelerating inflation and to real exchange rate appreciation. In the 1980s, and in the face of deteriorating terms of trade, both countries abandoned exchange rate fixity. Their experience indicates that terms of trade shocks may have severe consequences for output or inflation, and exchange rate flexibility may be an important means of cushioning those shocks.[22] Even in these circumstances, however, the advantages of flexibility have to be weighed against the other considerations discussed below.

Credibility of Anti-Inflationary Monetary Policy

A central argument in favor of fixed nominal exchange rates is that they may impose ''discipline'' on domestic monetary and fiscal policies and thereby enhance the country's ability to achieve price stability.[23] It is important here to distinguish between countries with and those without strong anti-inflationary credibility. The latter can easily justify pegging to the currency of a country with an established reputation for price stability as a means of disciplining both the authorities and the private sector. If credibility can be so established, it is likely to induce favorable changes in the structure of the economy, including lowering the risk premium in domestic interest rates and increasing the flexibility of wage-price determination.

In this situation, exchange rate stability is not in conflict with the objective of price stability; on the contrary, it becomes the *means* by which the low-credibility country establishes a nominal anchor to achieve price stability. Credibility for such a hard currency policy is not likely to be achieved costlessly or instantaneously. In a transition period there may be output costs in the face of domestic or external shocks. However, the credibility of the authorities and of the exchange rate commitment depends on convincing the private sector that the authorities are willing to bear those costs. Ultimately, when credibility has been established, the economy may function more efficiently, and exhibit lower average unemployment for a given inflation rate.

A classic illustration of this monetary policy strategy is provided by the experience of the European Monetary System (EMS) in the early 1980s. Since disinflation was then the priority in virtually all EMS countries and since Germany had the best reputation for price stability, there was a commonality of interests in trying to converge to the German inflation rate. Monetary policy in Germany thus served as the anchor of the system. While to date there have been 12 realignments (since

the beginning of the EMS in 1979), none of them has resulted in a revaluation relative to the deutsche mark, thereby leaving intact Germany's reputation as an exporter of credibility; also, these realignments have usually not fully compensated for past inflation differentials—so that the resulting real appreciation for higher-inflation countries acts as a disincentive to inflation.[24]

The need to ensure the credibility of monetary policy is at the heart of the debate over proposals for a European central bank. An EC intergovernmental conference is currently considering ways of achieving full economic and monetary union among member countries. Such a union would involve a movement to irrevocably fixed exchange rates (and perhaps to a single currency) and the implementation of a common monetary policy by a supranational institution. The key to designing this institution is to ensure that it continues to place an absolute priority on price stability, as does the Deutsche Bundesbank, and that it is both de jure and de facto immune from political pressures for monetary financing or indirect subsidies.

Non-EMS countries in Europe may also benefit from an implicit or explicit exchange rate peg. The benefits depend inversely on the extent to which the central bank is independent and its monetary policy already credible. The comparison of Switzerland and Austria is instructive. The Austrian schilling since 1981 has virtually been pegged to the deutsche mark, while Switzerland has targets for money growth and thus allows wider exchange rate fluctuations vis-à-vis the deutsche mark; interest differentials relative to Germany have tended to be more variable for Switzerland than for Austria (Chart 2). It has also been argued that de facto independence of the central bank is greater in Switzerland than in Austria.[25] Despite the difference in policy regime, outcomes in terms of inflation have been very similar (and similar to Germany's); the average rate of consumer price inflation over 1954–89 and 1981–89 was 4.1 percent and 3.6 percent, respectively, in Austria and 3.3 percent and 3.2 percent, respectively, in Switzerland, well below that for most other industrial countries (see Table 2). The key is monetary discipline, however it is achieved.

In Nordic countries, pegs to baskets of currencies have also helped to provide an anchor for monetary policies. From the late 1970s until recently, Sweden, Norway, and Finland all pegged to baskets whose weights

---

[22] Blundell-Wignall and Gregory (1990).

[23] Without such discipline, pegging to a strong currency would merely convert a noncredible monetary policy into a noncredible exchange rate policy. The effect of the exchange rate regime in disciplining fiscal policy is explored in Frenkel and Goldstein (1988b).

[24] If exchange rate realignments are ruled out, gaining competitiveness implies achieving a lower inflation rate than that of the anchor country for a time. Ungerer and others (1990) find that there is no systematic tendency for Germany to gain competitiveness relative to its exchange rate mechanism (ERM) partners when data for unit labor costs over the period since 1979 are considered.

[25] Genberg (1990). He quotes the Austrian National Bank's 1985 Annual Report to the effect that one reason for adopting the hard currency policy was to make ''. . . economic policy as a whole . . . less subject to pressures to take discretionary measures. . . .''

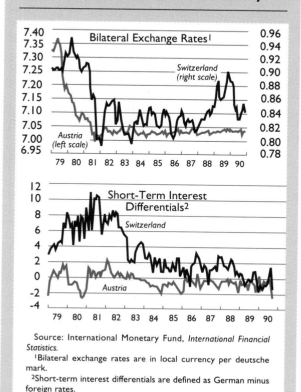

Chart 2. Austria and Switzerland: Bilateral Exchange Rates and Short–Term Interest Rate Differentials Relative to Germany

Source: International Monetary Fund, *International Financial Statistics.*

[1]Bilateral exchange rates are in local currency per deutsche mark.

[2]Short-term interest differentials are defined as German minus foreign rates.

Regional Integration

Greater fixity of exchange rates among groups of countries has typically accompanied regional moves to greater economic integration. A case in point is the EC, where economic and political integration has proceeded rapidly in the past and will progress further in the future—aided by the creation of a single European market for goods and services, moves to harmonize legislation, and the removal of exchange controls. It is natural in this context for greater fixity of exchange rates to emerge from greater monetary integration; the creation of the EMS in 1979 and recent proposals of the Delors Committee to move to completely fixed exchange rates are reflections of this.

There has been a two-way interaction between regional integration and exchange rate fixity within Europe. Chart 3 shows a secular increase in trade among EC countries as a percentage of their total trade—albeit with some leveling off in the 1974–85 period, associated with an increase in the value of oil trade owing to price increases by the Organization of the Petroleum Exporting Countries (OPEC). With the expansion of trade within the EC, the costs of uncertainty related to fluctuating exchange rates have been magnified. Various policy initiatives also rely on a common unit of

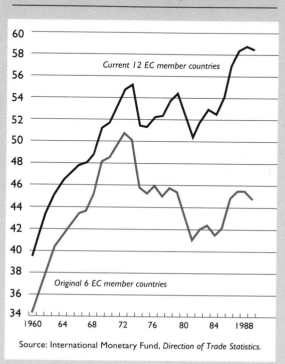

Chart 3. Share of Intra-EC Trade as a Percentage of Total Trade, 1960–89

Current 12 EC member countries

Original 6 EC member countries

Source: International Monetary Fund, *Direction of Trade Statistics.*

reflected bilateral trade, but with certain modifications, including the exclusion of nonconvertible currencies by Sweden and Finland, and, since 1982, the use of multilateral weights by Norway. During 1990 and 1991, a decision was made in each of the three countries to peg to the European currency unit (the ECU), a basket of EMS currencies. Fixity of exchange rates has helped to moderate wage increases; however, the authorities have retained a measure of flexibility, both in the composition of the currency baskets and also in the peg itself.[26] In particular, there were sizable depreciations in the 1977–82 period. It has been argued that the management of the adjustable peg in these three countries achieved the desired goal of relatively low unemployment, though at the cost of higher inflation than the average for industrial countries.[27]

---

[26]Gylfason (1990).

[27]Gylfason (1990). Average consumer price inflation in Sweden, Norway, and Finland in the periods 1954–89 and 1981–89 was 6.4 percent and 7.4 percent, respectively; compare Table 2 above.

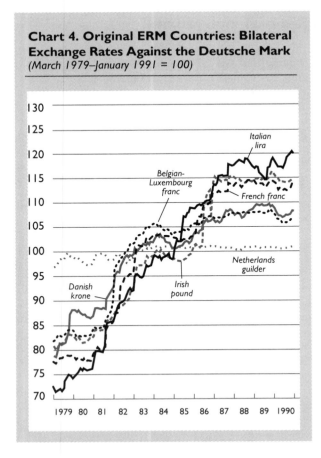

Chart 4. Original ERM Countries: Bilateral Exchange Rates Against the Deutsche Mark
(March 1979–January 1991 = 100)

account: distortions are created if market exchange rates diverge too much from those rates. Conversely, the existence of EC supranational institutions and shared objectives has made it easier to progress toward monetary integration, since compromises are easier to achieve when negotiations range across a number of areas. Chart 4, which plots the exchange rates of ERM currencies against the deutsche mark since the formation of the

EMS in March 1979, shows that exchange rate fluctuations have been reduced since 1982, as a result of less frequent realignments.

Economic integration in other regions is also proceeding. Within North America, two-way trade—which is already substantial because Canada and the United States are each other's largest trading partners—should be further stimulated by the Canada-U.S. Free Trade Agreement; free trade with Mexico is currently under discussion. Exchange rate fluctuations have also been much smaller between the U.S. dollar and the Canadian dollar than between the U.S. dollar and other major currencies, in particular the deutsche mark and the yen (Chart 5). In Asia, there has been a considerable increase in intraregional trade and direct investment among Japan, the newly industrializing economies (NIEs), and other economies of Southeast Asia. Japan and its Asian neighbors now have substantial trade links (Table 6), albeit within a more geographically diversified overall trade pattern than in Europe. Japanese direct investment in the rest of Asia (roughly the figure under "other countries" in Table 7) has been important, though it has increased less rapidly in recent years than has direct investment in the United States.

At this stage no one can know with any confidence whether the international monetary system will evolve in a "tri-polar" direction. The outcome will depend as much on political developments as on economic ones and will reflect decisions taken across a wide spectrum of countries, as exemplified by recent dramatic developments in Eastern Europe. As part of their overall efforts to stabilize their economies and to reorient them toward a more market-oriented structure of resource allocation, these countries will have to choose which exchange arrangements best meet their needs. This choice involves decisions not only on the desired degree of fixity of exchange rates but also on convertibility, on potential anchors for policy discipline, and on implications of changing trade patterns for reserves and for exchange rate management.

Table 6. Non-Fuel Merchandise Trade Matrix, 1985
(In billions of U.S. dollars)

	To			
	United States and Canada	Japan and Asian NIEs	European Community	Other
From				
United States and Canada	(98.7)	43.3	48.4	78.6
Japan and Asian NIEs	117.1	(62.7)	37.7	78.8
European Community	66.8	22.4	(312.5)	185.1
Other	41.8	31.0	84.2	(98.5)

Source: United Nations data on exports. Figures in parentheses show intercountry trade within the regional grouping.

Chart 5. Daily Percentage Changes in the U.S. Dollar Exchange Rates, January 1988–February 1991

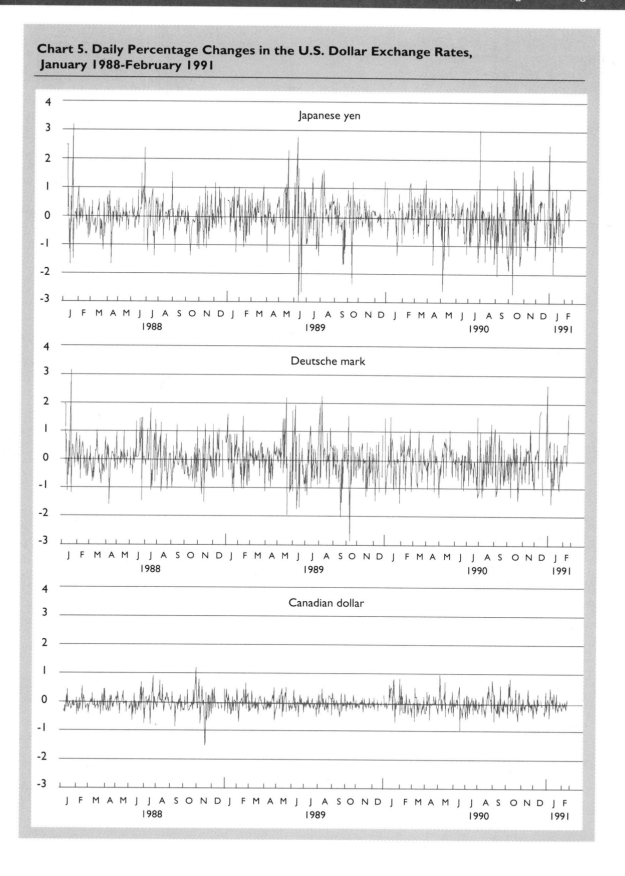

Table 7. Japan: Direct Investment Outflows and Inflows, 1982–90
(In millions of U.S. dollars)

| | | To or From: | | | | | |
| | | OECD countries | | | | Other countries | |
	All countries	United States	EC countries	Others	Communist bloc	Southeast Asia	Others
1982 Outflows	4,540	1,618	609	578	0	1,735	
Inflows	439	195	40	177	—	27	
1983 Outflows	3,612	1,326	604	285	1	1,396	
Inflows	416	285	66	8	—	57	
1984 Outflows	5,965	3,087	769	207	20	1,882	
Inflows	−10	−93	49	37	—	−3	
1985 Outflows	6,452	2,557	1,534	420	58	1,883	
Inflows	642	514	54	103	1	−30	
1986 Outflows	14,480	7,973	2,748	649	96	3,014	
Inflows	226	199	54	14	—	−41	
1987 Outflows	19,519	9,641	3,594	1,682	183	4,419	
Inflows	1,165	623	118	−23	—	447	
1988 Outflows	34,210	18,969	5,793	3,030	606	2,688	3,124
Inflows	−485	−599	100	42	2	−17	−13
1989 Outflows	44,130	21,238	9,746	4,532	713	5,005	2,896
Inflows	−1,054	−1,530	327	50	—	91	8
1990[1] Outflows	53,374	32,348	9,374	4,324	598	4,678	2,052
Inflows	2,006	980	756	58	2	170	40

Source: Bank of Japan, *Balance of Payments Monthly*, various issues.
[1] First half, annual rates.

V Exchange Market Stability as a Public Good

Thus far, the discussion has suggested that a successful international monetary system would have the following characteristics. First, it would have a nominal anchor that rested on the commitment of the largest industrial countries to domestic price stability. Second, it would embrace neither the view that "all current account imbalances should be eliminated" nor the view that "current accounts don't matter"; instead, it would seek to facilitate international adjustment by encouraging countries to eliminate undesirable and unsustainable external imbalances at the source. Third, it would allow for different degrees of exchange rate flexibility (and different exchange rate regimes) across countries, depending on structural characteristics of economies, the advantages of an external discipline for monetary policy, and incentives to regional integration.

Combining the first and third characteristics suggests that exchange rate commitments will be looser and quieter (that is, not involving publicly announced, narrow exchange rate ranges or targets) in the largest industrial countries than in smaller, more open economies—some of which may eventually even opt to join regional currency areas. But such a suggestion still leaves unanswered a key question: how will the system ensure that the major currencies—which after all have the greatest impact on the rest of the world—are not subject to serious misalignments and/or excess volatility? In other words, how can one obtain ". . . a more appropriate meshing of national sovereignty and international responsibilities"[28] now that the international community has come to regard exchange market stability as a public good that has a positive feedback on economic performance?

In seeking to promote exchange market stability, the larger industrial countries would assume a set of responsibilities. First and foremost, by setting the stance of monetary and fiscal policy on a stable, noninflationary course and by endeavoring to correct bad external imbalances at their source, they would provide a more stable focus for exchange rate expectations.[29]

The issue is not whether misalignments on the order of 1983–85 can recur; it is whether they can recur when fiscal policy is better disciplined and when external imbalances are much smaller. More disciplined policies would go a long way toward more disciplined exchange markets; the coordination of *policies* is therefore the key element of the ongoing coordination process in the Group of Seven. Second, authorities in these countries would regularly develop their own (quiet) estimates of equilibrium real exchange rates. These estimates may well be subject to substantial margins of uncertainty. Nevertheless, unless one accepts the view that the "market rate is always the right rate," an independent evaluation is needed. Third, in those (hopefully unusual) cases where there is a "large" difference between the market rate and official views of the equilibrium rate consistent with fundamentals, authorities would intervene. This intervention could take the form of a statement of official views on the desirable direction of exchange rate movements, of concerted, sterilized exchange market intervention, and—when necessary—of coordinated adjustments in monetary policies.[30] The Plaza Agreement and its aftermath is a good example. These responsibilities are contingent upon strong evidence of bubbles or large misalignments in exchange markets.

The responsibility to calm financial markets in periods of turbulence may be especially important today, as a result of increased integration of global financial markets. Underlying this increased integration have been a number of interrelated trends and processes, often summarized under the headings of liberalization, globalization, securitization, and innovation. Since these trends have been described in detail elsewhere,[31] it is enough here simply to mention the highlights. They include:

- the dismantling of capital controls and of limitations on entry of foreign financial institutions into the domestic market;

---

[28]Camdessus (1988a, p. 237).

[29]The fact that the largest countries have started the 1990s with a significantly better inflation performance than they did in the 1980s should itself be a positive factor.

[30]Persistent misalignments might also indicate the need to examine the appropriateness of other policies—in particular, fiscal and structural policies.

[31]International Monetary Fund (1987), Ogata, Cooper, and Schulmann (1989), and Chouraqui, Driscoll, and Strauss-Kahn (1988).

- the deregulation of interest rates on deposit, lending, and investment instruments, in favor of more market-determined levels;

- the rapid growth of offshore financial markets, removal of exchange controls, development of 24-hour screen-based global trading, and increased use of national currencies outside the country of issue;

- a shift toward use of direct debt markets and away from indirect finance, the packaging of assets not normally traded into tradable securities, and the creation of exchange-traded futures and options markets;

- a blurring of separations between commercial banking on the one hand and investment banking and security houses on the other; and

- the creation of a host of new financial products, ranging from currency and interest swaps, to floating rate notes, to note-issuance facilities.

Increased capital market liberalization increases the potential risks of beggar-thy-neighbor practices. The shift away from credit rationing and quantitative restrictions on lending means that the transmission mechanism of monetary policy falls more on "market prices," namely, on exchange rates and interest rates—the "competitive" variables most often cited in beggar-thy-neighbor complaints. Coordination is a way of discouraging such practices, and would likely involve increased exchange rate commitments.

Although such exchange rate commitments by the larger countries would be looser than in many target zone schemes, they would not necessarily be less effective. The stabilizing effect of any official exchange rate commitment on expectations depends on its *credibility*. One can argue that a looser commitment, wherein authorities react only to large, clear-call misalignments and do not claim that the primary assignment of monetary policy is for external balance, will be more credible than a (nominally) tighter and louder commitment. In evaluating the credibility of a commitment, market participants are also apt to weigh the costs of exchange rate instability against the costs of reduced monetary control. For the largest economies, the costs of reduced monetary control are perceived to be large enough to tip the balance in favor of exchange rates only when exchange markets are seriously misbehaving.

An exchange rate system that exhibits less hegemony and greater diversity of exchange arrangements than did the Bretton Woods system is not likely to function well unless an effective policy coordination process is in place (see Section VI). The absence of a single, dominant leader for the system implies that the assignment of responsibilities will be less obvious—and the structure of decision making more interdependent—than before. In fact, the ongoing policy coordination process in the Group of Seven can be characterized as a pragmatic response to *shared* leadership. Similarly, the diversity of exchange arrangements probably makes it more difficult to write "rules of the game" for the system that have wide applicability and yet are specific enough to make noncompliance transparent. The "peer pressure" associated with policy coordination can act to encourage responsible behavior and to compensate for any surfeit of guidance from existing codes of conduct. Without coordination, there would be greater danger that the "poles" of the international monetary system—and the countries grouped around them—might implement policies that would have negative spillover effects on other countries. As the experience of the 1980s has shown, such negative spillovers can arise not merely from misaligned exchange rates and financial market volatility but also—and more fundamentally—from undisciplined fiscal, structural, and monetary policies.

A response that should be avoided would be to attack the symptoms, rather than the fundamental causes, of misalignments and volatility. For instance, one strategy would be to throw "sand in the wheels" of the international capital markets by accepting restrictions or transactions taxes on capital flows. This strategy is based on the assessment that such restrictions would be less costly to the real side of the economy than either subordinating macroeconomic policies to exchange rate targets, or accepting the kinds of exchange rate fluctuations associated with greater policy autonomy.[32] There are at least four serious objections to such a strategy.[33]

First, to be effective, these proposals have to be widely implemented. Yet there is always an incentive for some country to capture more of the world's business by not imposing the tax. The globalization of capital markets means of course that it will be easier for consumers of financial services to find substitutes for taxed services elsewhere. If only the geographic location of speculation changes—and not its volume or nature—little will be accomplished.

Second, too little is known about asset-price behavior in markets with different levels of transactions taxes to be confident that it will penalize only bad speculators and socially unproductive capital flows—without affecting good ones.[34] For example, are asset-price volatility and misalignments systematically lower in, say, real estate markets (with high transactions costs) than in financial markets (with lower ones)? Are bubbles less prevalent in fine art and wine markets (where again transactions costs are relatively high) than in stock markets? If restrictions or taxes are not successful in separating productive from unproductive flows, we sacrifice some of the benefits of liberalization, including in-

---

[32]Tobin (1978).
[33]Frenkel and Goldstein (1988a).
[34]Mussa (1989).

creased returns to savers, a lower cost of capital to firms, and better hedging instruments against a variety of risks.

Third, restrictions on capital flows—even if they affected bad flows more than good ones—could weaken support for "outward-looking" policies and could spread to other areas, including the foreign trade sector.

Fourth, once sand has been thrown in the wheels, it may be difficult to get it out, as rent-seeking groups coalesce around the restrictions.

Nevertheless, the liberalization and globalization of capital markets have been accompanied by certain systemic risks, and some official action may be needed to reduce these risks. While this topic extends beyond the scope of this paper, two problems can be mentioned.[35]

A largely uncoordinated restructuring of capital markets can be unstable because of perverse incentives for risk-taking by financial institutions. While private market participants were exploiting the greater opportunities for arbitraging regulatory and fiscal differences across national and international jurisdictions, financial authorities were not reducing—in fact, they were significantly expanding—implicit and explicit liquidity and

solvency guarantees to these participants. If this process is not to create incentives for excessive risk-taking nor to lead to an undue transfer of private credit risk to the public sector, a more coordinated (and probably, harmonized) approach to prudential regulation will be needed. The recently concluded Basle agreement on risk-weighted capital standards for international banks is a good example of a cooperative solution to a problem generated by a competitive approach to bank regulation.

A second problem is that weaknesses in clearance and settlement systems could transform a local financial disturbance into a systemic crisis. Over the past decade, while improvements have made it possible to execute, say, a cross-border equity trade in minutes, clearance and settlement after the execution have not kept pace. Clearance and settlement of foreign currency transactions lean on international netting arrangements and hence have a supranational character. Systemic risk derives from the credit extended in interbank transactions during the settlement period. At issue is whether private cooperative arrangements can reduce systemic risk to acceptable levels when their capacity to discipline members and to provide them with liquidity is limited. Joint undertakings by the public and private sectors may be needed, along with a coordinated approach by central banks and other regulatory bodies.

---

[35]These problems are treated more comprehensively in Folkerts-Landau (1990).

VI Rationale for Policy Coordination

Previous sections have raised the issue of the need for policy coordination; in this section we step back and take a general look at the rationale for it, as well as at doubts about its effectiveness.[36]

The most logical starting point is to ask why international policy coordination would be beneficial in the first place. After all, if in the domestic economy the working of the invisible hand under pure competition translates independent decentralized decisions into a social optimum, why should the same principle not apply to policy decisions by countries in the world economy?

The answer is that economic policy actions, particularly those of larger countries, create quantitatively significant spillover effects or *externalities* for other countries, and that a global optimum requires that such externalities be taken into account in the decision making. Coordination is then best seen as a facilitating mechanism for internalizing these externalities.

This conclusion can perhaps be better appreciated by emphasizing the departures from the competitive model in today's global economy. Cooper (1987) has identified several such departures, and his analysis merits some extension here.

Unlike the atomistic economic agents of the competitive model that base their consumption and production decisions on prices that are beyond their control, larger countries exercise a certain degree of influence over prices, including the real exchange rate. This of course raises the specter that they will manipulate such prices to their own advantage and at the expense of others. Two examples are frequently cited—one dealing with inflation, and the other with real output and employment. Under floating rates, a Mundellian (1971) policy mix of tight monetary and loose fiscal policy allows an appreciated currency to enhance a country's disinflationary policy strategy—but at the cost of making it harder for trading partners to realize their own disinflation targets. Similarly, under conditions of high capital mobility and sticky nominal wages, a monetary expansion under floating rates leads to a real depreciation and to an expansion of output and employment at home. But the counterpart is that output and employ-

ment contract abroad.[37] Seen in this light, the role of coordination is to prevent—or to minimize—such intentional as well as unintentional beggar-thy-neighbor practices. Most international monetary constitutions have injunctions against "manipulating" exchange rates or international reserves.

The existence of public goods—and their role in resolving inconsistencies among policy targets—constitute a second important point of departure from the competitive model. When there are n currencies, there can be only n-1 independent exchange rate targets. Similarly, as discussed above, not all countries can achieve independently set targets for current account surpluses.

Adherents of decentralized policymaking—sometimes rather inappropriately labeled the "German school"—argue that such inconsistencies do not justify intervention.[38] Much as in the competitive model, the economic system will generate signals—in the form of changes in exchange rates, interest rates, prices, and incomes—that will lead to an adjustment of targets such that they eventually become consistent. If, however, the path to consistency involves large swings in real exchange rates, or, even more problematically, the imposition of restrictions on trade and capital flows, then reliance on decentralized policymaking may not be globally optimal. That a certain degree of stability in real exchange rates and an open international trading and financial system are valued in and of themselves (that is, they are public goods) is implicit in this conclusion. (In contrast, the market signals that resolve supply/demand inconsistencies in the competitive model

---

[36]This section draws on Frenkel, Goldstein, and Masson (1988).

[37]The conclusion that monetary expansion under floating rates affects real output in opposite directions at home and abroad is associated with the Mundell (1971)-Fleming (1962) model. For a recent evaluation of this model, see Frenkel and Razin (1987); a broader survey of the international transmission mechanism can be found in Frenkel and Mussa (1985). Econometric models are more divided on whether a monetary expansion under floating rates has negative transmission effects on real output abroad; see Helliwell and Padmore (1985) and Bryant and others (1988).

[38]We regard the label as inappropriate, both because the proponents of decentralized macroeconomy policymaking—including Corden (1983, 1986), Feldstein (1988), Niehans (1988), Stein (1987), and Vaubel (1985)—are geographically quite diverse, and because some prominent German economists, such as Pöhl (1987), have stressed the importance of coordination.

are not regarded as public goods.) If that is accepted, there is a positive role for coordination, both to identify target inconsistencies at an early stage and to resolve them in ways that do not produce too little of the public good(s).[39] It is of course possible for groups of countries who value the public good highly to attempt to obtain more of it by setting up regional zones of exchange rate stability or of free trade, and some have done just that (see the discussion in Section IV).[40] But the essence of a public good is that it will tend to be undersupplied so long as some large suppliers or users act in a decentralized fashion.

Once we leave the realm of atomistic competitors and enter the realm of nontrivial spillovers of policies—whether those spillovers occur in goods, assets, or labor markets—national governments may not be as effective in achieving their objectives independently as when their policies are coordinated with other governments.[41] A popular example illustrates this point. Whereas any single country acting alone may be reluctant to follow expansionary policies designed to counter a global deflationary shock for fear of unduly worsening its external balance, coordinated expansion by many countries will loosen the external constraint and permit each country to move closer to internal balance.

All of this establishes a *presumption* that there can be valid reasons for deviating from the tradition of decentralized decision making when it comes to economic policy, that is, that there is scope for coordination. This presumption is reinforced by two empirical observations. First, the world economy today is considerably more open and integrated than it was in 1950, or 1960, or even 1970. Not only have simple ratios of imports or exports to GNP increased, but also—and probably more fundamentally—global capital markets are more integrated.[42] With larger spillovers, there is more at stake in how one manages interdependence. Second, it is by now widely recognized that the insulating properties of floating exchange rates are more modest than was suspected prior to their introduction in 1973.[43]

But a presumption that cooperation could be beneficial is not the same as a guarantee—nor does it preclude the existence of sometimes formidable obstacles to its implementation.

Suppose national policymakers have a predilection for inflationary policies but are restrained from implementing them by the concern that relatively expansionary monetary policy will bring on a devaluation (or depreciation). Yet, as outlined by Rogoff (1985), if all countries pursue such inflationary policies simultaneously, none has to worry about the threat of devaluation. Here, coordination may actually weaken discipline by easing the balance of payments constraint. Similarly, as noted by Feldstein (1988), there is the potential risk that a coordinated attempt to stabilize a pattern of nominal or real exchange rates could take place at an inappropriately high aggregate rate of inflation, hence the concern for establishing a nominal anchor, as discussed in Section II. Equally troublesome would be a coordination of fiscal policies that yielded an aggregate fiscal deficit for the larger countries that put undue upward pressure on world interest rates. The basic point is straightforward: there is nothing in the coordination process that reduces the importance of sound macroeconomic policies.[44] There can be coordination around *good* policies and coordination around *bad* ones—just as with the exchange rate regime, where there are good fixes and bad fixes and good floats and bad floats.[45] Welfare improvements are not automatic.

It is only realistic, too, to acknowledge that there are barriers to the exercise of coordination. Four of the more prominent ones are worth mentioning.[46] First, international policy bargains that involve shared objectives can be frustrated if some policy instruments are treated as objectives in themselves. Schultze (1988), for example, offers the view that it would have been difficult to have reached a bargain on target zones for exchange rates in the early 1980s given President Reagan's twin commitments to increased defense spending and cutting taxes. In some other countries, the constraints on policy instruments may lie in different areas—including structural policies—but the implications are the same.

Second, countries can at times have sharp disagreements about the effects that policy changes have on policy targets. These differences may extend beyond the size to include even the sign of various policy-impact multipliers.[47] The harder it is to agree on how the world works, the harder it is to reach agreement on a jointly designed set of policies. This point is discussed

[39] Corden (1986) has argued that there may be a case for asking large countries to slow their speed of adjustment to desired policy targets so as to dampen movements in real exchange rates that could cause difficulties for others.

[40] Another constraint on regional attempts to create more of the public good is that they may divert or discourage its production outside the region; the argument here is analogous to the concepts of ''trade creation'' and ''trade diversion'' in the customs union literature.

[41] To reach this conclusion, it is necessary to assume that each player does not have sufficient policy instruments to achieve all its policy targets simultaneously, and that coordination alters the trade-offs among policy targets; see Gavin (1986). Without those assumptions, the motivation for coordination would disappear.

[42] See Fischer (1987), Frenkel (1983, 1986), and Section IV above.

[43] See Goldstein (1984). This is not to say that the insulating properties of floating rates are inferior to those of alternative regimes. Indeed, it is hard to see any other exchange rate regime surviving the shocks of the 1970s without widespread controls on trade and capital.

[44] See Bockelmann (1988) for a similar conclusion.

[45] See Frenkel (1985).

[46] Another barrier is disagreement over forecasts for key economic variables over the medium term; on this point, see Tanzi (1988).

[47] See Bryant and others (1988) and Helliwell and Padmore (1984) for a comparison of open-economy multipliers from different global econometric models.

further in Appendix I, where it is argued that, in fact, uncertainty may provide an incentive to coordinate policies internationally.

Third, whereas most countries have experienced a marked increase in openness over the past few decades, huge cross-country differences in the degree of interdependence remain. Large countries (the United States being the classic example) are generally less affected by other countries' policies than small ones. Coordination is not a matter of altruism, but rather the manifestation of mutual self-interest. To the extent that large countries are less beset by spillovers and feedbacks than small ones, the incentive of the former to coordinate on a continuous basis may be lower.[48] In this regard, the high degree of trade interdependence shared by members of the EMS can be seen as a positive factor in reinforcing incentives to coordinate in that group.

Finally, as Polak (1981) has reminded us, international bargaining typically comes after domestic bargaining. More specifically, the compromise of growth and inflation objectives at the national level may leave little room for further compromise on demand measures at the international level.

These barriers to coordination should not be overestimated: one of the clearest examples of true coordination—the Bonn economic summit of 1978—occurred just when domestic bargaining over the same issues was most intense;[49] the growing integration of capital markets—of which the global stock market crash of October 1987 is but one reminder—has brought home even to large countries the implications of interdependence; and continued empirical work on multicountry models should be able progressively to whittle down the margin of disagreement on the effects of policies.[50] If the scope of coordination is to expand beyond the efforts of the past, these obstacles will need to be overcome.

---

[48] See Fischer (1987). Dini (1988) argues further that when the incentives to coordinate differ widely among group members, there may be a tendency for *bilateral* bargains to take place among those who have the most to trade.

[49] See Putnam and Bayne (1984). At the same time, the Bonn summit is regarded in some quarters as illustrative of the pitfalls of coordinating macroeconomic policies when the economic outlook is changing rapidly.

[50] Appendix II gives a preliminary evaluation of some simple coordination rules using the Fund's model, MULTIMOD.

VII Role of the Fund

As stated in the Articles of Agreement, a primary purpose of the International Monetary Fund is to provide "the machinery for consultation and collaboration on international monetary problems."[51] That business is carried out in Article IV consultation discussions, in discussions by the Executive Board and the Interim Committee of the staff's *World Economic Outlook*, in the Board's informal sessions on exchange rate developments, in Board discussions of policy papers dealing with the desired evolution of the system, and in the assistance provided by the IMF to the Group of Seven policy coordination exercise. In the broadest terms, the relevance of these multilateral surveillance activities of the Fund for the exchange rate system is that they all are directed at moving countries toward better macroeconomic and structural policies. Alternative exchange rate arrangements are different in how they seek to discipline policies but they are not so different in the kind of policy discipline that is required to make each of them work well. Surveillance can thus be seen as a mechanism that should reinforce the operation of the exchange rate system.

The need for multilateral surveillance increases with the growth in interdependence and the integration of international capital markets. In such a world, bad policies taken by a large country have smaller domestic effects but larger external ones. Moreover, high capital mobility may permit bad policies to continue longer, even if they are ultimately unsustainable. This possibility makes it especially important for the repercussions of policies to be carefully analyzed in a timely fashion.

The Fund is in a good position to provide such analysis from a global perspective—in part by applying economic indicators and analyzing alternative medium-term scenarios. As suggested earlier, a host of thorny analytical issues will continue to arise in overseeing the functioning of the exchange rate system. These include: how to check the consistency of targets that large countries have for internal balance; how to estimate the "adding-up" effects of large countries' monetary and fiscal policy stances; how to distinguish "desirable" from "undesirable" external imbalances; how to evaluate the relative costs of alternative ways of correcting undesirable imbalances; and how best to estimate equilibrium real exchange rates.

The Fund also has a major responsibility for ensuring that the functioning of the exchange rate system is not impaired by the composition of international liquidity or by the terms and conditions under which it is provided. The SDR was created to supplement existing sources of international liquidity—reserve currencies and gold. A number of recent discussions have considered a variety of proposals and approaches for using the SDR to strengthen the functioning of the system, but none has elicited sufficient support to break "the impasse in the role of the SDR."[52]

This impasse raises the question of whether the existing allocation criterion has lost its operational usefulness, given that the Articles of Agreement also call for making the SDR the principal reserve asset in the international monetary system. Profound changes would of course have to be made in the system before the SDR could fulfill that function—changes that would inevitably take considerable time to bring about.

In the interim, the key issue of whether it is prudent to let the SDR shrink further as a share of reserve portfolios remains.[53] As the Managing Director has pointed out: (1) reliance on borrowed reserves is now greater than it used to be; (2) instability in financial markets and shifts in market confidence in individual countries are unlikely to fade away in the period ahead; (3) mechanisms that facilitate the financing of coordinated exchange market intervention can help to counter disruptive speculative forces in exchange markets; and (4) generating reserves solely through further adjustment of current account positions can be very costly for many countries—particularly when overlaid on the broad withdrawal of commercial banks from lending to many developing countries.[54] In each of these areas, one can question whether the SDR cannot play a more important role than it is now doing, so as to improve the functioning and stability of the international monetary system.

---

[51] Article I(i).

[52] Polak (1988).

[53] At the end of August 1990, SDR holdings represented 3.3 percent of the nongold reserves of all countries, based on totals in *International Financial Statistics*.

[54] Camdessus (1988b).

Appendix I   Economic Policy Coordination in Context of Uncertainty

An important aspect of policy coordination is the lack of knowledge about the effects of policies and hence whether a particular policy choice is likely to have beneficial, or harmful, effects.[55] For instance, Feldstein (1988) has argued

> Uncertainties about the actual state of the international economy and uncertainties about the effects of one country's policies on the economies of other countries make it impossible to be confident that coordinated policy shifts would actually be beneficial (p. 10).

Evidence of the lack of knowledge about the effects of policies can be gleaned from a comparison of existing multicountry models that has been made at the Brookings Institution (see Bryant and others (1988)). The second-year multiplier effects on GDP of a standardized increase in government expenditure in the United States ranged from 0.4 to 2.1, while the transmission effects on GDP in the rest of the Organization for Economic Cooperation and Development (OECD) area ranged from slightly negative to 0.7. Moreover, estimates of single parameters—for instance, the interest elasticity of investment or the direct substitution effect of government spending on private consumption—often have very large standard errors relative to estimated coefficients.

Lack of knowledge about the functioning of the world economy—which we will term *model uncertainty*—should be distinguished from *disagreement* about the correct view of the world, which may or may not involve the recognition by policymakers that their view of the world may not be correct.[56] In an extreme case, each policymaker may be convinced that he has the truth, but that the others do not. In such a case, each may think that he can fool the others into reaching agreements that they think are in their best interest but are not. Disagreement among policymakers is discussed below, but let us first consider the question of model uncertainty.

Model Uncertainty

A natural way to treat model uncertainty is to formulate a general model that includes the various possible models (assuming that they constitute a relatively small set) as special cases with different parameter values—that is, treat model uncertainty as parameter uncertainty. If we can formulate the problem as finding the optimal policies (either coordinated or uncoordinated) in the presence of ranges of possible parameter values, then the analysis of Brainard (1967) applies. He shows that in general there is a trade-off between close attainment of targets and increases in the variance of the target variable. For instance, suppose that, starting from a situation where policy is set to hit a target exactly, an oil price shock threatens to produce a suboptimal outcome; should an attempt be made to use the policy instrument to counteract fully the effect of the shock? Since the effect of the policy instrument is uncertain, doing so may in fact more than offset the effect of the shock. The main lesson from Brainard (1967) is that policy should be less activist in the presence of model uncertainty, and should not attempt to respond fully to shocks.[57] In other words, policymakers in general should not engage in fine-tuning of policy instruments.

What is the lesson for the gains that may result from international coordination of policies? On the surface, policy coordination may seem to be more activist than independent pursuit of policy goals by the countries concerned, but that presumption is not correct. On the contrary, policy coordination may rule out certain types of activist policies, such as the use of the exchange rate in a beggar-thy-neighbor fashion as in competitive depreciation to generate employment or in appreciation to achieve quick disinflation. The question is whether the existence of uncertainty increases the gap between coordinated policies (which, by definition, are fully optimal if problems of time inconsistency are ruled out) and uncoordinated policies.

---

[55]This appendix draws on Frenkel, Goldstein, and Masson (1991).

[56]It is of course true that a high degree of model uncertainty is likely to be associated with disagreement about the functioning of the world economy.

[57]This conclusion may not apply to general models where there are many targets and instruments, however. We are indebted to David Kendrick for this point.

There is a useful distinction between uncertainty about the effects of policies in the country taking the action (which we will call *domestic multiplier uncertainty*) and uncertainty about the effects on the home country of policy moves taken abroad (which we will call *transmission multiplier uncertainty*). In the former, no general results emerge as to whether an increase in uncertainty will increase or decrease gains from policy coordination. In the latter, there is an unambiguous increase in the gap between coordinated and uncoordinated policies, and hence an increase in the gains from policy coordination (Ghosh and Ghosh (1991), Ghosh and Masson (1988)). Uncoordinated policies, because they do not correctly capture the endogenous nature of *foreign* policymaking (that is, the reaction of policy abroad to moves taken at home), do not properly take into account this element of uncertainty, which is larger the greater is the variance of transmission multipliers. Coordinated policies, in contrast, internalize this aspect of uncertainty. Thus, ex ante gains from policy coordination may be larger than is suggested by the simulation of deterministic models that use point estimates of parameter values and ignore uncertainty.

This conclusion emerges from the model simulations performed by Ghosh and Masson (1988), in which a two-country global model of the United States versus the rest of the world was used to quantify gains from policy coordination. Ranges for parameters were established from a survey of empirical work, and three possible models were considered: a midpoint estimate, and the high and the low extremes of the range. Policymakers (and private agents) were all assumed to assign the same probabilities to these possible models, and to set optimal policy on the basis of expected utility maximization. It was shown that uncertainty in most parameters increased the gain from choosing policy in a coordinated fashion relative to independent utility maximization—that is, uncertainty increased expected gains from policy coordination.

A recent instance—the stock market crash of October 1987—may help to solidify the argument and illustrate its real-world relevance. It could be argued that the shock to stock prices also produced greater uncertainty about underlying transmission mechanisms. The central banks were concerned at the time of the crash that liquidity should be increased, to avoid the risk of bankruptcies by investment houses and a crisis of confidence in the real economy. However, a central bank acting alone runs the risk that by increasing the money supply and lowering interest rates, it may provoke a run against the currency, exacerbating financial collapse. In such circumstances, the absence of cooperation among monetary authorities may lead them to increase liquidity by less than the optimal amount; therefore, the uncertainty about effects on exchange markets should be an incentive for enhanced coordination. Of course, the need for coordination depends on the nature of the shocks and the perceived risks. Paradoxically, the fact that the shift out of equities into other assets was generalized across major countries may have minimized the need for coordination in October 1987.

Disagreement About Models

Uncertainty may or may not be associated with disagreement among policymakers about the ''correct'' representation of reality. If policymakers disagree (and one or both is therefore necessarily wrong), then, as Frankel and Rockett (1988) point out, coordination agreements may lead to losses ex post, rather than to gains, relative to uncoordinated policymaking. They calculate that coordination between the United States and the rest of the OECD is about as likely to worsen welfare as to improve it, when models are chosen from those represented in the comparison of models made at the Brookings conference cited above, and where coordination involves setting policies to maximize joint utility (assumed to depend on both regions' output and inflation performance).

The significance of this result has been questioned on two grounds. First, coordination is unlikely if one of the partners to an agreement believes that the other is using the wrong model, and that in fact the agreed policies will be demonstrably worse for that country than the alternative, uncoordinated policy (Holtham and Hughes Hallett (1987)). In this case, there is the danger that the agreement might be abandoned by one of the parties. In addition, the perception that one of them had taken advantage of the other might preclude later beneficial cooperation. By ruling out some of the cases considered by Frankel and Rockett (1988), the conclusion that coordination has a good chance of being harmful is considerably weakened. In Frankel (1991), the calculation is redone for only those bargains that improve both countries' welfare under either of the models the two countries believe in: if the ''true'' model is chosen from the full set of 10 models, as before, coordination now improves U.S. welfare in 78 percent of the cases, and rest-of-OECD welfare in 76 percent of them.

The second qualification is to suggest that the models probably do not adequately represent the nature of disagreements among the policymakers. Ghosh and Masson (1991) start from alternative estimated variants of a standard two-country open-economy model (Oudiz and Sachs (1984)), which contains about the same degree of reduced-form multiplier uncertainty as the models considered by Frankel and Rockett. They show that if policymakers learn from observations on endogenous variables about the probabilities to be assigned to each of the models, using Bayesian learning, the subjective probabilities converge rather quickly to the objective ones. This result suggests that the experiment performed by Frankel and Rockett (1988) is rather artificial. It may be true that the range of disagreement among the models of the Brookings conference is in fact larger than that among policymakers—some of the models can clearly be ruled out. Alternatively, policymakers' views of reality may be much more subtle than those represented by the models—they are models after all—and policy setting cannot be represented by such simple optimization exercises.

Appendix II   Evaluation of Some Simple Coordinated Policy Rules

The gains from policy coordination have often been evaluated in the context of *optimal* policies when countries act jointly to determine their policies, compared with policies chosen optimally when countries act independently (see, for instance, various articles in Buiter and Marston (1985)). More relevant may be the comparison of simple rules that are not optimal in the context of any single model, but that may be more robust across a range of models, more credible to the general public, and easier to implement.[58]

In this appendix, we examine several simple rules that have been proposed, by simulating the Fund's MULTIMOD model.[59] The rules that we compare are money and nominal income targeting—rules that can be implemented by countries independently—and fixed nominal exchange rates, target zones, and current account targets—rules that require an element of coordination if implemented by all countries because such targets cannot be chosen independently. For example, if two countries target their bilateral exchange rate, the targets cannot be inconsistent; another example is current account balance targets, which must add up globally. Of course, many other forms of policy coordination are possible; for instance, Frankel (1990) has proposed coordinating around mutually agreed targets for nominal income in each of the major industrial countries.

We first consider the behavior of each of the rules in response to *individual* shocks (that is, to shocks to *individual* residuals). Each shock is assumed to be unanticipated when it occurs, and to be an innovation that applies to a single period. Though temporary, such shocks will nevertheless have persistent effects because errors in the model are serially correlated and because the various structural equations of the model contain dynamic effects. Expectations are assumed to be formed in the model in a way that properly takes into account the subsequent dynamics; that is, once the shock has occurred, perfect foresight is assumed to prevail.

The results from single shocks do not of course allow a complete evaluation of policy rules. In general, the relative variance of different kinds of shocks should

influence the choice between policy rules. Nevertheless, single-shock exercises can be useful because they allow a characterization of *when* particular rules are likely to perform better than others.

We follow the single-shock simulations with some *stochastic* simulations under which errors are consistent with their estimated distribution. One advantage of these stochastic simulations is that the variances of the shocks reflect their relative importance. A formal ranking of the policy rules would require an explicit objective function that specifies the weights to be given to output fluctuations, inflation, and to other objectives. We do not attempt to provide such a ranking, but rather suggest some strengths and weaknesses of each of the rules.

Form of the Reaction Functions

As a prelude to the simulation results, it is necessary to specify exactly how we implement the various policy rules in MULTIMOD. In brief, we imposed reaction functions for the short-term interest rate, assumed to be the instrument for monetary policy, and for real government spending on goods and services, assumed to be the fiscal policy instrument. Details of the feedback rules are given in Frenkel, Goldstein, and Masson (1989b).

The form of the policy rules requires some explanation because there is inevitably some element of arbitrariness in the way they are specified. In general, we have attempted to follow as closely as possible the intentions of their advocates. The final form chosen resulted from some experimentation that identified inadequacies with alternative specifications or with feedback parameters.

Money targeting, rule (1), used the same specification as in the standard version of MULTIMOD. To achieve exactly a money target would produce large swings in short-term interest rates. For that reason, the model includes an equation in which interest rates equate the long-run demand for money, conditional on observed GNP, with the money stock target.

Nominal GNP targeting, rule (2), was specified in terms of a target for the level of nominal income, rather than its rate of change, because of the potential insta-

---

[58]This appendix draws on Frenkel, Goldstein, and Masson (1989b).

[59]The version of the model used in these simulations is described in Masson and others (1988).

bility from targeting the latter, discussed in Taylor (1985). Some experimentation with feedback coefficients led to a value that yields a flatter aggregate demand schedule (in real output, price space) under nominal income targeting than under money targeting, again as in Taylor (1985).

Fixed nominal exchange rates, rule (3), were implemented by putting a large feedback coefficient on the deviation of the actual from the targeted nominal rate in the equation for short-term interest rates. Variations of exchange rates are thereby kept within narrow margins. It should be stressed that there is an asymmetry in the implementation of this rule as between the United States and other industrial countries. The latter are assumed to subordinate their monetary policies to maintaining dollar parities, whereas the United States is assumed to target monetary aggregates independently of exchange rate considerations, thereby providing a nominal anchor for the system.

Target zones, rule (4), follow as closely as possible the guidelines described in Williamson and Miller (1987) and simulated earlier (using the Federal Reserve Board's Multi-Country Model) by Edison, Miller, and Williamson (1987). We experimented with various values of the feedback coefficients to achieve the closest control over the targets without producing explosive behavior in the model. As in Edison and others, there is nothing that ensures that the real exchange rate will not in fact depart from the zone (if shocks are large enough). As described in Williamson and Miller (1987), a target for the level of world nominal income serves as the nominal anchor for prices. Note, however, that it is the level, not the rate of change, of world nominal income that appears in our equation;[60] the latter is subject to the criticisms made by Taylor (1985) for domestic targeting and did in practice produce problems of nonconvergence in MULTIMOD. The feedback coefficient on world nominal income implies that a 10 percent deviation from baseline raises world interest rates by 1 percentage point.

The *extended target zones or "blueprint" proposal*, rule (5), contains a policy reaction function for government spending as well as the target zone assignment of monetary policy to the real exchange rate. The equation that endogenizes fiscal expenditures is a feedback rule that aims to close a gap between domestic absorption and its target value. This rule does not hit domestic absorption exactly, but with the feedback coefficient that is imposed, deviations from absorption targets are typically small.

In implementing *reversed assignment*,[61] rule (6), we have specified that the short-term interest rate responds to the proportional gap between nominal absorption and

its target, whereas government spending responds strongly to the gap between the current account (as a ratio to GNP) and its target. Instrument instability does not seem to be a problem in the latter case; indeed, in principle, the feedback coefficient could be infinite, forcing deviations of current balances from targets to zero. However, the conclusions derived from the simulations are unlikely to be sensitive to the small deviations from current account targets that result from our specification. If anything, our simulations probably give too much weight to current account targets and not enough to nominal demand targets, and closer control of the latter might have been possible otherwise.

Simulations of Individual Shocks

Four individual shocks are considered:

(1) an aggregate *demand shock* in the United States: a positive innovation in consumption equal to 1 percent.
(2) an aggregate *supply shock* in the United States; in particular, the residual in the equation for the rate of change in the non-oil GNP deflator is increased by 2 percent.
(3) a *shift in demand* toward U.S. goods, equal to 10 percent of U.S. exports.
(4) a *portfolio preference shift* out of U.S. dollar assets, leading to an increase in the required rate of return on dollar assets by 10 percentage points.

Each of the rules is simulated subject to each of the four shocks, one at a time. The results are portrayed in Charts 6–9.

The aggregate demand shock, namely, a 1 percent increase in U.S. consumption,[62] has quite different effects under the different policy rules (Chart 6). Without any policy changes, such a shock will increase output and put upward pressure on prices, as well as appreciate the real exchange rate and lead to a decline in the current account. It also generates positive spillovers for the output of other countries. Since nominal GNP rises, as does the demand for money, both uncoordinated rules cause interest rates to rise; given the relative steepness of the aggregate demand curves, output and price increases are more moderate with nominal income targeting than with monetary targeting.

Under target zones, the real appreciation of the U.S. dollar leads to a smaller rise in interest rates in the United States than in other industrial countries. However, by limiting the interest rate increases in the United States in response to a demand increase, this rule builds in inflationary pressures, which persist longer than for

---

[60]Williamson and Miller (1987) are not specific about the form that this term should take.
[61]See Genberg and Swoboda (1987) and Boughton (1988).

[62]The error in this equation has a serial correlation coefficient equal to 0.148, so that roughly 15 percent of the shock persists into the second year, 2 percent into the third year, etc. See Appendix II, Table 3 of Frenkel, Goldstein, and Masson (1989b).

Chart 6. Shock to U.S. Consumption
(Deviations of U.S. variables from baseline)

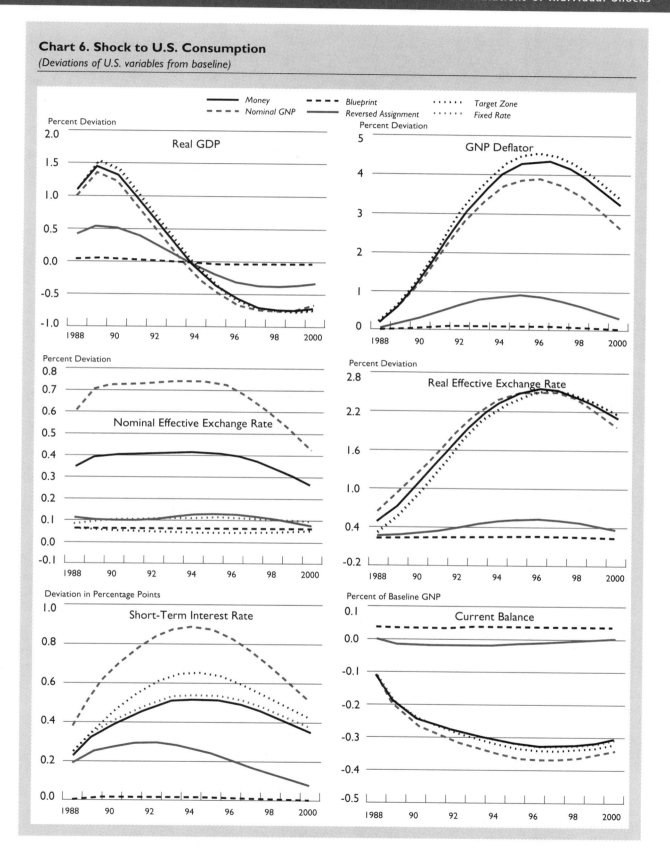

other rules. Fixed nominal exchange rates yield a similar outcome. In contrast, the extra degree of freedom accorded by fiscal policy in both the blueprint and the reversed assignment rules allows the aggregate demand shock to be almost completely offset by lower government spending. As a result, the output, price, and real exchange rate effects are smallest for these two rules. A comparison of the blueprint with the reversed assignment rule illustrates the relative effectiveness of monetary and fiscal policies. Government spending cuts can easily offset the effects of increased consumption on absorption, allowing the blueprint rule virtually to neutralize the shock. In contrast, control of nominal absorption through the interest rate is not as powerful, at least for values of feedback coefficients that do not produce large swings in interest rates or other variables.

The negative aggregate supply shock (or cost-push inflation shock) likewise yields a variety of responses (Chart 7). This shock has persistent effects because of considerable stickiness in the inflation process. In response to this stagflationary shock, nominal GNP targeting leads to a greater response of interest rates, and hence to greater short-run output losses but smaller increases in prices, than money targeting. Which of the two is preferable depends on the trade-off between the two objectives of output and price level stability, as well as on the discount rate that captures intertemporal trade-offs. Given the very small effects on exchange rates under all rules, fixed rates produce similar results to uncoordinated money targeting.

The responses under target zones and blueprint rules are another story. Using monetary policy to counteract the real appreciation of the U.S. dollar requires *lower*, not higher, U.S. nominal interest rates. However, for both the target zones and blueprint rules there is an additional term that tends to raise interest rates in all countries if world nominal income grows too fast, which happens here. The result with target zones is that U.S. interest rates rise, but by somewhat less than interest rates in other industrial countries. Price level increases continue longer, and are larger in the medium term, than for any other policy rule. It is also true that interest rates have to continue increasing for six years in response to a purely transitory supply shock because of the inertia in the inflation process.

In contrast, interest rates have to rise much less under the blueprint rule because government spending contracts, helping to limit the real appreciation of the dollar. The contraction of government spending is required because the increase in U.S. prices yields an improvement in the terms of trade, which raises real disposable income and stimulates consumption. Though the net effect on output is negative in the short run, output is actually higher after seven years, by which time prices have returned to their baseline levels. It is clear that an aggregate supply shock causes a dilemma for target zones because one instrument—monetary policy—has

to wear *two* hats—resisting inflationary pressures and limiting appreciation of the real exchange rate (in the country experiencing the shock).[63] The reversed assignment rule behaves much like the blueprint: both yield relatively small current balance effects.

Chart 8 illustrates the effects of an expenditure-switching shock that corresponds to a shift toward U.S. goods and away from other countries' goods. The positive shock to U.S. exports of 10 percent shows up in lower exports of other countries in proportions that correspond to their shares in world trade.[64] The U.S. current account improves by some 0.6–0.7 percent of GNP in the first period under all rules except reversed assignment, for which the current account change is smaller. For all policy rules, U.S. real output rises initially, and price increases are small. Since neither real exchange rates nor industrial country nominal GNP change much, there is little effect on interest rates under either fixed rates, target zones, or the blueprint.

In contrast, under the reversed assignment rule, the increase in the U.S. current account balance leads to *increased* U.S. Government spending, adding to the stimulus to U.S. output; conversely, government spending declines in other countries. Higher U.S. nominal GNP has to be resisted by higher U.S. interest rates, so that shifts in preferences between countries' goods lead to a shift in the monetary/fiscal mix under reversed assignment—to tighter monetary/looser fiscal policy in the country facing the increase in its exports, and conversely for those facing lower exports. The contrast between this rule and the others has been heightened by the large feedback coefficient on the current balance: attempts to exert tight control over the current account lead to large swings in other variables under reversed assignment.

The exchange rate shock (Chart 9) puts downward pressure on the dollar relative to the yen, to the deutsche mark, and to other industrial country currencies. The initiating factor is assumed to be a 10 percent increase in the required return on dollar assets.[65] Output effects are largest under reversed assignment and under the two uncoordinated rules (money and nominal GNP targeting)—and are smallest under the blueprint rule and fixed rates. The exchange rate always overshoots except under fixed rates, with the U.S. nominal effective exchange rate depreciating by about 15 percent in the first

---

[63] If there is no feedback of inflation on monetary policy—such as through world nominal income—then the target zones rule cannot be simulated, given the absence of a nominal anchor.

[64] The shock is distributed using the weights that serve to allocate the world trade discrepancy in MULTIMOD. As a result, the shock to the United States is also reduced by the U.S. share, so that U.S. exports rise on impact by about 8.6 percent, not the full 10 percent.

[65] As in the historical data, the risk premium shocks are quite persistent (owing perhaps to speculative bubbles as well as to shifts in portfolio preferences), with serial correlation coefficients equal to 0.43 for shocks to interest parity between the United States and Japan, and 0.75 between the United States and Germany.

Chart 7. U.S. Aggregate Supply Shock
(Deviations of U.S. variables from baseline)

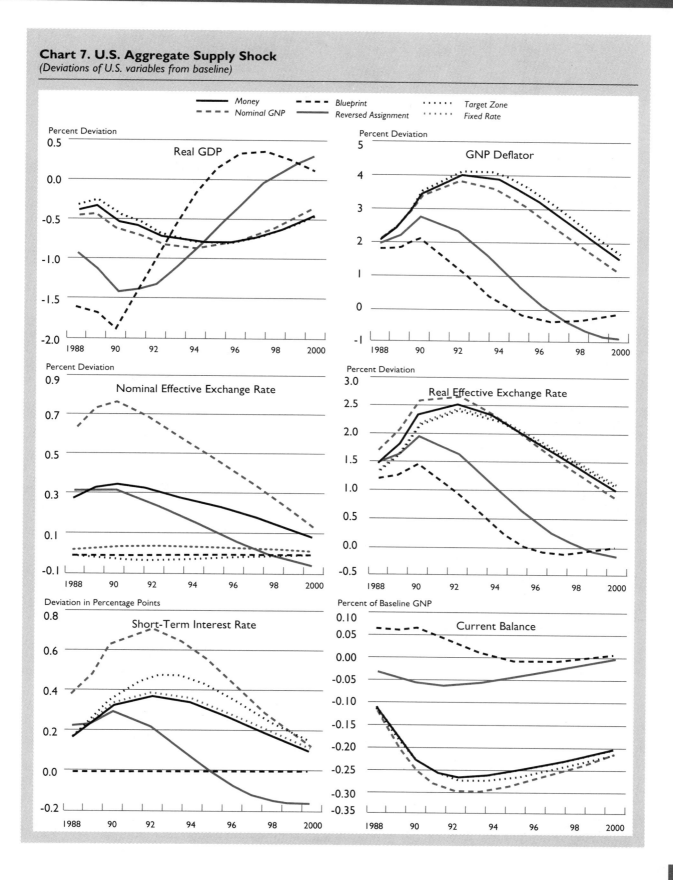

Chart 8. Shock to U.S. Exports
(Deviations of U.S. variables from baseline)

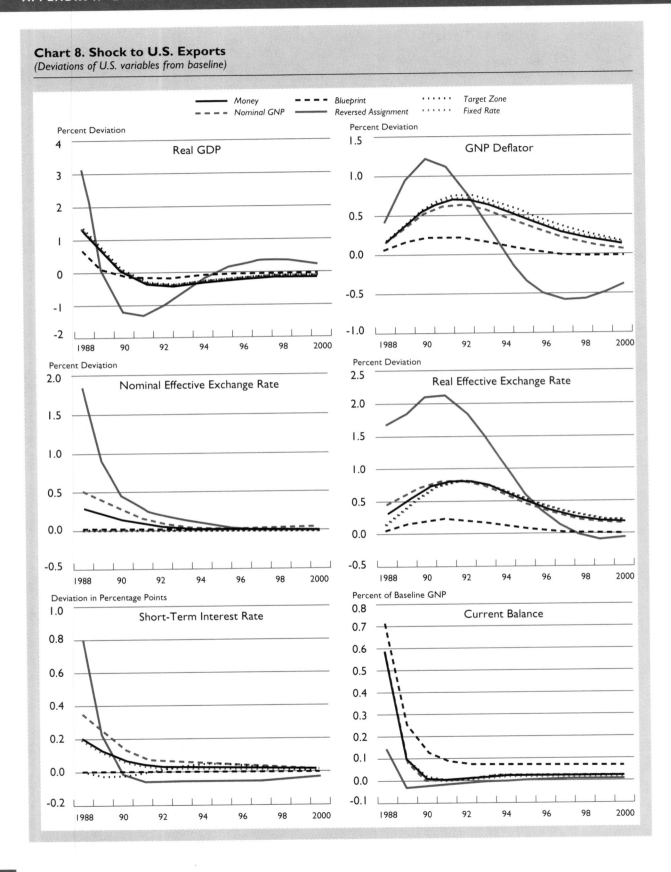

Chart 9. Shock to Value of U.S. Dollar
(Deviations of U.S. variables from baseline)

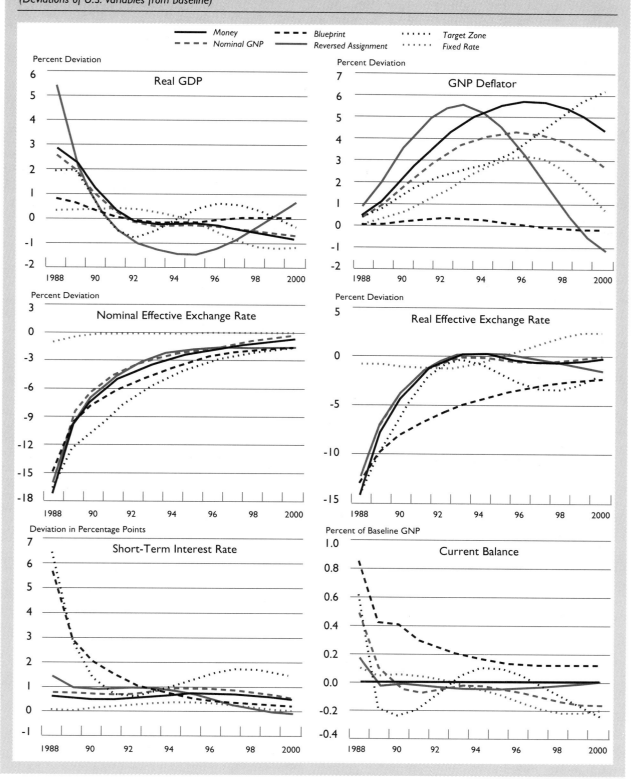

year. Under target zones, despite an initial increase of 6 percentage points in the short-term interest rate, the real effective exchange rate still depreciates considerably. Moreover, the behavior of the GNP deflator suggests that target zones can generate price level instability—a point we return to below in the context of stochastic simulations. Under reversed assignment, government spending *rises* because of the improvement in the U.S. current account; again, this additional stimulus tends to induce large movements in output.

A money demand shock was also examined. The results are not plotted because they are simple to describe. It is only with money targeting that the money shock has any significant effect on policy settings and on other endogenous variables (the money shock has a small effect on consumption because money is a component of net wealth, but the magnitude is negligible). Under money targeting, the positive innovation to money demand leads to temporarily higher short-term interest rates, and as a result, to lower economic activity for a time. Other policy rules ignore the money demand shock and maintain policy instruments unchanged, allowing macroeconomic variables to remain at their equilibrium levels. This demonstrates the superiority of these rules in the face of money demand shocks, an argument that has long been emphasized by advocates of nominal GNP targeting (for example, Tobin (1980)).

Stochastic Simulations

Simulations of individual shocks, though instructive, do not lend themselves to easy generalizations because no rule dominates the others for all kinds of shocks. It is clear that monetary policy rules (assumed to be credible, and fully understood by the private sector) are relatively ineffective, especially in affecting real variables. Rules using fiscal policy therefore have clear advantages in offsetting shocks, though the assumed flexibility for fiscal policy may be unrealistic. In addition, the proper assignment of monetary and fiscal policies to internal or external balance depends on the nature of shocks. We now turn to simulations where the variances of the shocks reflect their relative importance. Moreover, instead of applying shocks for one period only, we apply shocks in successive periods. By looking at a sufficient number of years, the model should provide useful information about the variances of endogenous variables under the alternative policy rules.

The simulations are performed on the assumption that expectations are formed rationally. The shocks (by definition) are unanticipated at the time they occur. In this context, rational expectations of variables in future periods are formed taking the expected value of those shocks—namely, zero.[66] In each period, however, a

drawing is made from the covariance matrix describing the shocks. The *realized* values of endogenous variables are affected by the shocks, and in general will differ from the expectations for those variables formed in previous periods.

The stochastic simulations involve multiple simulations. Not only is it necessary to iterate to a terminal date to force expectations to be consistent with the model's solution conditional on information available to time *t*, but it is also necessary to repeat the process each time a new drawing of shocks is made.

In the first set of stochastic simulations, for which root mean square (RMS) deviations from baseline are presented in Table 8, we use a drawing for the shocks that corresponds to residuals in the model's behavioral equations for 1974–85. These shocks are applied to a baseline for the period 1988–99; the model is simulated another 20 years to minimize the effect of the terminal conditions on the period of interest. The implicit objective is to minimize deviations of target variables from the baseline, so that shocks have as little disruptive effect as possible. We do not make a judgment about how target variables should be weighted in the objective function; however, we presume that macroeconomic performance would be evaluated using some subset of the variables presented in Table 8.[67]

Several conclusions emerge from examination of the results.

First, it appears that nominal GNP targeting produces smaller errors in response to typical shocks than money targeting. As noted earlier, nominal GNP targeting has a clear advantage over money targeting when there are shocks to velocity, that is, to the demand for money. For other kinds of shocks, the comparison between the two rules derives from small differences in the elasticity with respect to nominal income and in the speed with which the interest rate reacts to shocks. For the historical shocks considered here, the stabilization properties of the nominal income rule clearly dominated those of base money targeting.

Second, the two rules that ignore domestic variables in setting monetary policy in favor of targeting an exchange rate measure—while keeping fiscal expenditures exogenous—show mixed results: they have some success in reducing the variability of GDP for the United States and for developing countries, but yield no clear advantage for Germany and Japan.

---

[66]In fact, the model has to be linear for this to be fully consistent with rationality.

[67]It could be argued that the sole criterion should be the discounted utility of consumption, and the variances of variables would matter only insofar as they reduced the output available for consumption (or increased the variance of consumption itself). The model as currently specified does not incorporate such effects, making it necessary to evaluate rules on the basis of their effectiveness in reducing the variability of key variables. Of course, the absence in the model of links between second and first moments (that is, variances and means) of variables makes it subject to Lucas critique problems.

Table 8. Root Mean Square Deviations from Baseline for Various Policy Rules, Historical Shocks

			Policy Rule				
	Money targeting	Nominal GNP targeting	Fixed rate (1)	Fixed rate (2)	Target zone	Blueprint	Reversed assignment
United States							
Real GDP[1]	3.6	3.2	3.0	2.8	2.7	1.4	7.9
Inflation	3.0	2.3	3.4	3.0	1.7	0.8	3.2
Current balance[2]	0.7	0.7	0.6	0.6	0.4	0.5	0.2
Real effective exchange rate[1]	9.1	8.3	5.6	4.3	7.3	4.9	9.1
Nominal effective exchange rate[1]	7.2	8.1	0.3	0.1	7.0	5.8	5.8
Nominal interest rate	1.4	1.2	1.5	1.4	2.8	1.8	1.7
Japan							
Real GDP[1]	3.8	3.2	4.0	4.1	3.7	1.6	5.2
Inflation	5.8	4.8	4.8	4.3	4.1	1.7	3.9
Current balance[2]	0.6	0.6	0.5	0.5	0.5	0.8	0.2
Real effective exchange rate[1]	8.9	8.2	3.8	3.8	6.9	5.5	5.9
Nominal effective exchange rate[1]	11.9	9.8	0.5	0.1	11.8	10.1	11.8
Nominal interest rate	1.5	2.3	4.4	1.3	2.5	1.3	2.3
Germany							
Real GDP[1]	4.4	4.3	3.4	3.1	6.9	2.9	4.2
Inflation	3.7	3.0	4.9	4.2	2.9	2.4	2.2
Current balance[2]	1.4	1.4	1.0	1.0	0.1	2.2	0.6
Real effective exchange rate[1]	8.2	7.6	2.1	2.2	10.4	7.4	8.0
Nominal effective exchange rate[1]	11.9	8.5	0.4	0.0	16.3	14.2	11.8
Nominal interest rate	2.7	1.8	5.9	1.4	3.3	1.1	1.1
Developing Countries							
Real GDP[1]	3.4	3.4	3.2	1.3	2.1	1.6	1.5
Terms of trade[1]	5.5	5.1	5.6	5.1	4.5	2.5	3.7

[1] Root mean square percent errors.
[2] As a percent of GNP.

Note also that the behavior of macroeconomic variables is quite different under fixed nominal exchange rates—column (1)—than under target zones. Recall that fixed rates are implemented here through changes in monetary policies of industrial countries other than the United States. The United States is assumed to target the monetary base, as under monetary targeting. As a result, the variability of nominal interest rates is considerably higher abroad than in the United States. The fixity of nominal exchange rates is also associated with more variability of inflation in all industrial countries.

Some might argue that stochastic simulations of fixed rates using historical shocks overstate the need for movements in interest rates. Since the period 1974–85 was characterized by flexible exchange rates, a credible announcement of a set of nominal exchange rate targets could be seen as reducing shifts between currencies. Moreover, our earlier single-shock simulations suggested that target zones could be unstable under exchange rate shocks; response to such shocks could be unfavorably biasing the results against target zones. To examine this question, we also ran some simulations for which shocks to interest parity conditions were assumed to be absent.

These results—shown in column (2) under fixed rates—exhibit only slightly less variability. It does not seem therefore that our results are strongly affected by changes in speculative behavior in currency markets that might be associated with the exchange rate regime.

The target zones rule, in contrast to fixed nominal rates, posits a *symmetric* assignment of monetary policies to *real* effective exchange rates. As hinted at earlier, achievement of tight target zones is difficult in the model, and RMS deviations from baseline for real exchange rates are quite high; on the other hand, real GDP, at least in the United States, and inflation generally, are quite stable. The policy reaction functions for target zones used here are based on Edison, Miller, and Williamson (1987); our results suggest, however, that a more complicated rule for setting interest rates—perhaps using proportional, integral, and derivative control terms—would be more appropriate.[68] Such rules may also be more robust to model misspecification. At the same time, we would argue that the fact that a simple rule does not perform well suggests some skepticism about the practicality of real exchange rate targeting, given the uncertainty associated with the precise dynamics of the economy.

Third, the blueprint rule produces considerably lower errors for most variables,[69] but does so with the benefit of an additional policy instrument—namely, real government spending. Somewhat surprisingly, the reversed assignment rule does not succeed in stabilizing either real GDP (except for developing countries) or real effective exchange rates.[70] Though current account targets are achieved closely under reversed assignment, they may not be the preferred measure of external balance because shocks that change the terms of trade will change the valuation of trade flows for given trade volumes. Stabilizing the current balance will therefore not be sufficient to neutralize the domestic demand effects of external shocks.

Our historical shocks comprise a small sample—only 12 observations—and it does not seem appropriate to evaluate policy rules on the basis of one historical episode. Our second set of stochastic simulations therefore draws shocks for 61 residuals over 40 years from the distribution describing the historical shocks. The simulations were then performed as described above, one year at a time. Table 9 presents the RMS deviations from baseline for the various policy rules.

There are several qualitative differences relative to the historical shocks of Table 8. *First*, the ranking of money and nominal GNP targeting has changed. The reason seems to lie in the timing of shocks to developing country supplies of commodities and manufactured exports. In the historical simulations, these shocks occur mainly at the *end* of the simulation period; they have persistent effects, but since the RMS deviations are calculated only over the 12 years of the shocks, some of those effects are not captured. In contrast, the generated shocks distribute those effects more evenly over the simulation, and nominal GNP targeting, with its flatter aggregate demand curve, performs more poorly than money targeting.

Second, fixed rates in Table 9 no longer dominate the two uncoordinated rules with respect to real GDP in Japan, nor for the real effective exchange rate of the dollar. Unless a considerable premium is placed on *nominal* exchange rate stability, there seems little to choose among the first three rules—money and nominal GNP targets, and fixed rates. Unfortunately, the target zones proposal could not be simulated here; with the feedback parameters specified in Edison, Miller, and Williamson (1987), the target zone rule suffers from dynamic instability that eventually prevents MULTIMOD from converging to a solution. The problem is exacerbated by the longer simulation period, because real shocks push the short-run equilibrium real exchange rate further from its long-run equilibrium value.[71]

Third, the blueprint rule—column (1)—again seems to yield for most variables lower RMS deviations than the other rules. Its superiority, however, with respect to reversed assignment is less marked than in Table 8. As discussed above, both of these rules assume that real government spending can be flexibly used in the current period to respond to deviations from targets—be it nominal domestic demand (blueprint) or the current balance (reversed assignment). A more realistic assumption, in our view, would be that fiscal spending can respond with a *lag* of a year to deviations from targets. Taking account of this inflexibility would mean that lower (higher) growth in nominal domestic demand under the blueprint rule would lead to higher (lower) government spending in the *following* year. In our first attempt to make this constraint operational, we used the same feedback coefficients as in column (1); however, this produced dynamic instability. The results presented in column (2) use a feedback of nominal domestic demand onto government spending that is half of the contemporaneous effect. Interestingly enough, the RMS deviations for this variant of the blueprint rule are now

---

[68] Such specifications have been used by Currie and Wren-Lewis (1987, 1988a, 1988b), among others.

[69] Though it does not stabilize nominal effective exchange rates in Japan and Germany. Nominal effective exchange rates use MERM weights, and include only industrial country currencies, while *real* effective exchange rates are calculated using relative manufacturing export prices weighted according to export shares; developing countries are included in this calculation.

[70] Currie and Wren-Lewis (1988a) also find that such a rule performs less well than the blueprint assignment.

[71] Of course, given the assumption that agents know those values, policymakers could (in the model) have moving targets for exchange rates, trying only to offset current shocks, and not the lagged effects of past shocks. But such an experiment—which would in effect involve starting each period's simulation at baseline values—was not performed.

Table 9. Root Mean Square Deviations from Baseline for Various Policy Rules, Generated Shocks, 1988–2027

	Policy Rule					
	Money targeting	Nominal GNP targeting	Fixed rate	Blueprint (1)	Blueprint (2)	Reversed assignment
United States						
Real GDP[1]	5.1	5.4	5.0	1.9	3.2	4.4
Inflation	3.7	3.3	3.4	1.2	1.3	2.3
Current balance[2]	0.9	1.2	0.8	1.2	0.9	0.2
Real effective exchange rate[1]	11.6	12.8	11.8	6.3	5.7	7.6
Nominal effective exchange rate[1]	8.1	8.5	0.4	10.3	8.8	5.1
Nominal interest rate	2.0	4.0	1.6	1.4	1.7	1.7
Japan						
Real GDP[1]	5.2	6.0	5.8	2.9	5.9	4.4
Inflation	5.3	4.9	4.9	2.4	2.7	3.6
Current balance[2]	4.9	2.5	1.5	1.9	1.8	0.4
Real effective exchange rate	7.8	10.1	5.7	5.0	5.0	6.8
Nominal effective exchange rate	11.3	17.2	0.4	9.2	9.4	8.2
Nominal interest rate	2.3	2.8	3.7	0.9	1.1	2.0
Germany						
Real GDP[1]	5.1	4.5	3.8	3.5	4.4	4.8
Inflation	4.8	4.1	3.9	2.4	2.2	2.9
Current balance[2]	3.9	1.6	2.4	3.5	3.2	0.4
Real effective exchange rate[1]	8.4	6.6	6.1	7.4	6.4	9.8
Nominal effective exchange rate[1]	14.2	11.9	0.5	15.9	14.0	11.8
Nominal interest rate	2.8	3.0	6.3	1.5	1.3	2.2
Developing Countries						
Real GDP[1]	2.4	3.7	2.1	2.3	2.5	2.0
Terms of trade[1]	4.9	6.4	3.9	2.8	2.8	3.1

[1] Root mean square percent errors.
[2] As a percent of GDP.

closer to those for the other rules.[72] It is a topic for further research to examine the constrained use of fiscal policy to hit other targets—for instance, under the reversed assignment rule.

It should be stressed that simulation results for simple coordinated and uncoordinated policy rules should *not* be used to draw inferences about the effects of judg-

mental (discretionary) coordinated policies, including the ongoing coordination exercise among the largest industrial countries. In this connection, the differences between the effects of coordinated policy rules and judgmental coordinated policies may be as large as those between uncoordinated policy rules and coordinated policy rules. A key task of future research in this area should be to learn about the effects of judgmental policies—even though such policies do not lend themselves easily to simulation exercises.

[72]Except for current account balances. It seems that because of J-curves, the lagged response of government spending actually does better in offsetting the current account effect of most shocks.

References

Aghevli, Bijan B., Mohsin S. Khan, and Peter J. Montiel, *Exchange Rate Policy in Developing Countries: Some Analytical Issues,* IMF Occasional Paper 78 (Washington: International Monetary Fund, 1991).

Argy, Victor, and Paul De Grauwe, eds., *Choosing an Exchange Rate Regime: The Challenge for Smaller Industrial Countries* (Washington: International Monetary Fund, 1990).

Blundell-Wignall, Adrian, and Robert G. Gregory, "Exchange Rate Policy in Advanced Commodity-Exporting Countries: Australia and New Zealand," in *Choosing an Exchange Rate Regime: The Challenge for Smaller Industrial Countries,* ed. by Victor Argy and Paul De Grauwe (Washington: International Monetary Fund, 1990), pp. 224–71.

Bockelmann, H., "The Need for Worldwide Coordination of Economic Policies," paper presented at conference on "Financing the World Economy in the Nineties," School for Banking and Finance, Tilburg University, Netherlands, March 1988.

Boughton, James M., "Policy Assignment Strategies with Somewhat Flexible Exchange Rates," IMF Working Paper, WP/88/40 (May 1988).

————, and William H. Branson, "Commodity Prices as a Leading Indicator of Inflation," NBER Working Paper No. 2750 (Cambridge, Massachusetts: National Bureau of Economic Research, October 1988).

Bovenberg, Lans, "International Coordination of Tax Policies," Chap. 6 in *The Reality of International Economic Policy Coordination,* ed. by H.J. Blommestein (Amsterdam: North-Holland, forthcoming, 1991).

Brainard, William C., "Uncertainty and the Effectiveness of Policy," *American Economic Review,* Vol. 57 (May 1967), pp. 411–25.

Branson, William H., Jacob A. Frenkel, and Morris Goldstein, eds., *International Policy Coordination and Exchange Rate Fluctuations* (Chicago: University of Chicago Press, 1990).

Bryant, Ralph C., and others, eds., *Empirical Macroeconomics for Interdependent Economies* (Washington: The Brookings Institution, 1988).

Buiter, Willem H., and Richard C. Marston, eds., *International Economic Policy Coordination* (New York: Cambridge University Press, 1985).

Camdessus, Michel (1988a), "The Task for the Beginning of the 1990s," remarks before First International Frankfurt Bankers' Dinner, Frankfurt, June 30, 1988; reprinted in *IMF Survey,* July 11, 1988, pp. 237–39.

————(1988b), "The Evolving International Monetary System: Some Issues," 1988 C.D. Deshmukh Memorial Lecture, Bombay, October 4, 1988; reprinted in *IMF Survey,* October 31, 1988, pp. 338–40.

Chouraqui, Jean-Claude, Michael Driscoll, and Marc-Olivier Strauss-Kahn, "The Effects of Monetary Policy on the Real Sector: An Overview of Empirical Evidence for Selected OECD Economies," Working Paper 51 (Paris: Organization for Economic Cooperation and Development, 1988).

Cooper, Richard N., "The Gold Standard: Historical Facts and Future Prospects," *Brookings Papers on Economic Activity: 1* (1982), The Brookings Institution, pp. 1–56.

————, "International Economic Cooperation: Is It Desirable? Is It Likely?" IMF Seminar Series No. 1987–10 (Washington, October 29, 1987).

Corden, W. Max, "The Logic of the International Monetary Non-System," in *Reflections on a Troubled World Economy: Essays in Honour of Herbert Giersch,* ed. by Fritz Machlup, Gerhard Fels, and Hubertus Muller-Groeling (New York: St. Martin's Press, 1983), pp. 59–74.

————, "Fiscal Policies, Current Accounts and Real Exchange Rates: In Search of a Logic of International Policy Coordination," *Weltwirtschaftliches Archiv,* Vol. 122, No. 3 (1986), pp. 423–38.

Crockett, Andrew, and Morris Goldstein, *Strengthening the International Monetary System: Exchange Rates, Surveillance, and Objective Indicators,* Occasional Paper 50 (Washington: International Monetary Fund, 1987).

Currie, David A., and Simon Wren-Lewis, "Conflict and Cooperation in International Macroeconomic Policymaking: The Past Decade and Future Prospects" (unpublished; International Monetary Fund, December 1987).

————(1988a), "A Comparison of Alternative Regimes for International Macropolicy Coordination," London Business School, Discussion Paper No. 07–88.

————(1988b), "Evaluating the Extended Target Zone Proposal for the G-3," Centre for Economic Policy Research, Discussion Paper No. 221 (January 1988).

Dini, Lamberto, "Cooperation and Conflict in Monetary and Trade Policies," International Management and Development Institute, U.S.-European Top Management Roundtable, Milan, February 19, 1988.

Edison, Hali J., Marcus H. Miller, and John Williamson, "On Evaluating and Extending the Target Zone Proposal," *Journal of Policy Modeling,* Vol. 9 (Spring 1987), pp. 199–224.

Feldstein, Martin, "Distinguished Lecture on Economics in Government: Thinking About International Economic Coordination," *Journal of Economic Perspectives,* Vol. 2 (Spring 1988), pp. 3–13.

Fischer, Stanley, "International Macroeconomic Policy Co-ordination," NBER Working Paper No. 2244 (Cambridge, Massachusetts: National Bureau of Economic Research, May 1987).

Fleming, J. Marcus, "Domestic Financial Policies Under Fixed and Under Floating Exchange Rates," *Staff Papers*, International Monetary Fund, Vol. 9 (November 1962), pp. 369–79.

Folkerts-Landau, David, "The Case for International Coordination of Financial Policy," in *International Policy Coordination and Exchange Rate Fluctuations,* ed. by William H. Branson, Jacob A. Frenkel, and Morris Goldstein (Chicago: University of Chicago Press, 1990), pp. 279–306.

Frankel, Jeffrey, "Obstacles to Coordination, and a Consideration of Two Proposals to Overcome Them: International Nominal Targeting (INT) and the Hosomi Fund," in *International Policy Coordination and Exchange Rate Fluctuations,* ed. by William H. Branson, Jacob A. Frenkel, and Morris Goldstein (Chicago: University of Chicago Press, 1990), pp. 109–45.

————, "A Note on Internationally Coordinated Policy Packages Intended to Be Robust Under Model Uncertainty" (unpublished; Berkeley, California: University of California, March 1, 1991).

————, and Katharine E. Rockett, "International Macroeconomic Policy Coordination when Policymakers Do Not Agree on the True Model," *American Economic Review*, Vol. 78 (June 1988), pp. 318–40.

Frenkel, Jacob A., "International Liquidity and Monetary Control," in *International Money and Credit: The Policy Roles,* ed. by George M. von Furstenberg (Washington: International Monetary Fund, 1983), pp. 65–109.

————, "A Note on 'the Good Fix' and 'the Bad Fix'," *European Economic Review*, Vol. 28 (June/July 1985), pp. 125–27.

————, "International Interdependence and the Constraints on Macroeconomic Policies," *Weltwirtschaftliches Archiv*, Vol. 122, No. 4 (1986), pp. 615–46.

————, and Michael L. Mussa, "Asset Markets, Exchange Rates, and the Balance of Payments," Chap. 14 in *Handbook of International Economics,* ed. by Ronald W. Jones and Peter B. Kenen, Vol. 2 (Amsterdam; New York: North-Holland, 1985).

Frenkel, Jacob A., and Assaf Razin, "The Mundell-Fleming Model a Quarter Century Later: A Unified Exposition," *Staff Papers*, International Monetary Fund, Vol. 34 (December 1987), pp. 567–620.

Frenkel, Jacob A., and Morris Goldstein (1988a), "Exchange Rate Volatility and Misalignment: Evaluating Some Proposals for Reform," in *Financial Market Volatility*, proceedings of a symposium sponsored by the Federal Reserve Bank of Kansas City, Jackson Hole, Wyoming, August 17–19, 1988 (Kansas City, Missouri: Federal Reserve Bank of Kansas City, 1988).

————(1988b), "The International Monetary System: Developments and Prospects," *Cato Journal*, Vol. 8 (Fall 1988), pp. 285–306.

————, and Paul R. Masson, "International Coordination of Economic Policies: Scope, Methods, and Effects," in *Economic Policy Coordination,* Wilfried Guth, moderator (Washington: International Monetary Fund; Hamburg: HWWA-Institut für Wirtschaftsforschung, 1988).

————(1989a), "International Dimensions of Monetary Policy: Coordination Versus Autonomy," in *Monetary Policy Issues in the 1990s*, proceedings of a symposium sponsored by the Federal Reserve Bank of Kansas City, Jackson Hole, Wyoming, August 30–September 1, 1989 (Kansas City, Missouri: Federal Reserve Bank of Kansas City, 1989).

————(1989b), "Simulating the Effects of Some Simple Coordinated Versus Uncoordinated Policy Rules," in *Macroeconomic Policies in an Interdependent World*, ed. by Ralph Bryant and others (Washington: International Monetary Fund, 1989), pp. 203–39.

————, "Key Issues in the International Coordination of Economic Policies," Chap. 2 in *The Reality of International Economic Policy Coordination*, ed. by Hans J. Blommestein (Amsterdam: North-Holland, forthcoming, 1991).

Gavin, Michael, "Macroeconomic Policy Coordination Under Alternative Exchange Rate Regimes" (unpublished; Federal Reserve Board, September 1986).

Genberg, Hans, "In the Shadow of the Mark: Exchange Rate and Monetary Policy in Austria and Switzerland," in *Choosing an Exchange Rate Regime: The Challenge for Smaller Industrial Countries*, ed. by Victor Argy and Paul De Grauwe (Washington: International Monetary Fund, 1990), pp. 197–219.

————, and Alexander K. Swoboda, "The Current Account and the Policy Mix Under Flexible Exchange Rates," IMF Working Paper, WP/87/70 (October 1987).

Ghosh, Atish R., and Swati Ghosh, "Does Model Uncertainty Really Preclude International Policy Coordination?" *Journal of International Economics* (forthcoming, 1991).

Ghosh, Atish R., and Paul R. Masson, "International Policy Coordination in a World with Model Uncertainty," *Staff Papers,* International Monetary Fund, Vol. 35 (June 1988), pp. 230–58.

————, "Model Uncertainty, Learning and Gains from Coordination," *American Economic Review,* Vol. 81 (June 1991), pp. 465–79.

Goldstein, Morris, *The Exchange Rate System: Lessons of the Past and Options for the Future,* IMF Occasional Paper 30 (Washington: International Monetary Fund, July 1984).

————, and others, *Determinants and Systemic Consequences of International Capital Flows* , IMF Occasional Paper 77 (Washington: International Monetary Fund, 1991).

Greenspan, Alan, Statement Before the Subcommittee on Domestic Monetary Policy of the Committee on Banking, Finance and Urban Affairs of the House of Representatives, October 25, 1989, in *Zero Inflation: Hearing on H.J. Res. 409*, 101st Cong., 1st Sess. (Washington: U.S. Government Printing Office, 1990).

Guth, Wilfried, moderator, *Economic Policy Coordination,* Proceedings of an international seminar held in Hamburg, May 1988 (Washington: International Monetary Fund; Hamburg: HWWA-Institut für Wirtschaftsforschung, 1988).

Gylfason, Thorvaldur, "Exchange Rate Policy, Inflation, and Unemployment: The Nordic EFTA Countries," in *Choosing an Exchange Rate Regime: The Challenge for*

Smaller Industrial Countries, ed. by Victor Argy and Paul De Grauwe (Washington: International Monetary Fund, 1990), pp. 163–92.

Hamada, Koichi, "Alternative Exchange Rate Systems and the Interdependence of Monetary Policies," in *National Monetary Policies and the International Monetary System,* ed. by R.Z. Aliber (Chicago: University of Chicago Press, 1974), pp. 13–33.

Heller, H. Robert, "Anchoring the International Monetary System," address before the International Economic Working Group in Washington, March 24, 1987.

Helliwell, John F., and Tim Padmore, "Empirical Studies of Macroeconomic Interdependence," Chap. 21 in *Handbook of International Economics,* ed. by Ronald W. Jones and Peter B. Kenen, Vol. 2 (Amsterdam; New York: North-Holland, 1985), pp. 1107–51.

Holtham, Gerald, and Andrew Hughes Hallett, "International Policy Coordination and Model Uncertainty," in *Global Macroeconomics: Policy Conflict and Cooperation,* ed. by Ralph Bryant and Richard Portes (London: Macmillan, 1987), pp. 128–77.

International Monetary Fund, *Annual Report* (Washington: International Monetary Fund, 1990).

McKinnon, Ronald I., *An International Standard for Monetary Stabilization,* Policy Analyses in International Economics, No. 8 (Washington: Institute for International Economics, 1984).

Masson, Paul R., Steven Symansky, Richard Haas, and Michael Dooley, "MULTIMOD—A Multi-Region Econometric Model," *Staff Studies for the World Economic Outlook* (Washington: International Monetary Fund, July 1988), pp. 50–104.

Meltzer, Allan H., "Some Evidence on the Comparative Uncertainty Experienced under Different Monetary Regimes," in *Alternative Monetary Regimes,* ed. by Colin D. Campbell and William R. Dougan (Baltimore: Johns Hopkins University Press, 1986), pp. 122–53.

Mundell, Robert A., *The Dollar and the Policy Mix,* Essays in International Finance, No. 85 (Princeton, New Jersey: Princeton University Press, May 1971).

Mussa, Michael, "Transactions Taxes as a Cure for Asset Price Volatility and Misalignment: Some Preliminary Thoughts" (unpublished; University of Chicago, March 1989).

Niehans, Jürg, "Generating International Disturbances," in *Toward a World of Economic Stability: Optimal Monetary Framework and Policy,* ed. by Yoshio Suzuki and Mitsuaki Okabe (Tokyo: University of Tokyo Press, 1988), pp. 181–218.

Ogata, Shijuro, Richard N. Cooper, and Horst Schulmann, *International Financial Integration: The Policy Challenges* (New York: Trilateral Commission, 1989).

Oudiz, Gilles, and Jeffrey Sachs, "Macroeconomic Policy Coordination Among the Industrial Economies," *Brookings Papers on Economic Activity: 1* (1984), pp. 1–75.

Pöhl, Karl Otto, "Cooperation—A Keystone for the Stability of the International Monetary System," First Arthur Burns Memorial Lecture, at the American Council on Germany, New York, November 2, 1987.

Polak, Jacques J., *Coordination of National Economic Policies,* Group of Thirty, Occasional Paper No. 7 (New York: Group of Thirty, 1981).

_____ , "The Impasse Concerning the Role of the SDR," in *The Quest for National and Global Economic Stability,* ed. by Wietze Eizenga, E. Frans Limburg, and Jacques J. Polak (Dordrecht, Netherlands: Kluwer Academic Publishers, 1988).

Putnam, Robert D., and Nicholas Bayne, *Hanging Together: The Seven-Power Summits* (Cambridge, Massachusetts: Harvard University Press, 1984).

Rogoff, Kenneth, "Can International Monetary Policy Cooperation be Counterproductive?" *Journal of International Economics,* Vol. 18 (May 1985), pp. 199–217.

Schlesinger, Helmut, "Comment on Polak's Economic Policy Objectives and Policymaking in the Major Industrial Countries," in *Economic Policy Coordination,* Wilfried Guth, moderator (Washington: International Monetary Fund; Hamburg: HWWA-Institut für Wirtschaftsforschung, 1988).

Schultze, Charles L., "International Macroeconomics Coordination—Marrying the Economic Models with Political Reality," in *International Economic Cooperation,* ed. by Martin Feldstein (Chicago: University of Chicago Press, 1988).

Stein, Herbert, "International Coordination of Economic Policy," *The AEI Economist* (Washington: The American Enterprise Institute, August 1987).

Suzuki, Yoshio, "International Monetary Cooperation: Is it Necessary? If So, How?" paper presented to the Konstanz Conference, Switzerland, May 25, 1989.

Tanzi, Vito, "Fiscal Policy and International Coordination: Current and Future Issues," paper presented at Conference on Fiscal Policy, Economic Adjustment, and Financial Markets, Bocconi University, January 27–30, 1988.

Taylor, John, "What Would Nominal GNP Targeting Do to the Business Cycle," in *Understanding Monetary Regimes, Carnegie-Rochester Conference Series on Public Policy,* ed. by Karl Brunner and Allan H. Meltzer, Vol. 22 (Amsterdam: North-Holland, 1985), pp. 61–84.

Tobin, James, "A Proposal for International Monetary Reform," Cowles Foundation Discussion Paper, No. 506, Cowles Foundation for Research in Economics (New Haven: Yale University Press, 1978).

_____ , "Stabilization Policy Ten Years After," *Brookings Papers on Economic Activity: 1* (1980), pp. 19–71.

Ungerer, Horst, Jouko J. Hauvonen, Augusto Lopez-Claros, and Thomas Mayer, *The European Monetary System: Developments and Perspectives,* IMF Occasional Paper 73 (Washington: International Monetary Fund, 1990).

Vaubel, Roland, "International Collusion or Competition for Macroeconomic Policy Coordination? A Restatement," *Recherches Economiques de Louvain,* Vol. 51 (December 1985), pp. 223–40.

Watson, Maxwell, and others, *International Capital Markets: Developments and Prospects, January 1988* (Washington: International Monetary Fund, 1988).

Williamson, John, and Marcus H. Miller, *Targets and Indicators: A Blueprint for the International Coordination of Economic Policy,* Policy Analyses in International Economics, No. 22 (Washington: Institute for International Economics, 1987).

Recent Occasional Papers of the International Monetary Fund

82. Characteristics of a Successful Exchange Rate System, by Jacob A. Frenkel, Morris Goldstein, and Paul R. Masson. 1991.

81. Currency Convertibility and the Transformation of Centrally Planned Economies, by Joshua E. Greene and Peter Isard. 1991.

80. Domestic Public Debt of Externally Indebted Countries, by Pablo E. Guidotti and Manmohan S. Kumar. 1991.

79. The Mongolian People's Republic: Toward a Market Economy, by Elizabeth Milne, John Leimone, Franek Rozwadowski, and Padej Sukachevin. 1991.

78. Exchange Rate Policy in Developing Countries: Some Analytical Issues, by Bijan B. Aghevli, Mohsin S. Khan, and Peter J. Montiel. 1991.

77. Determinants and Systemic Consequences of International Capital Flows, by Morris Goldstein, Donald J. Mathieson, David Folkerts-Landau, Timothy Lane, J. Saúl Lizondo, and Liliana Rojas-Suárez. 1991.

76. China: Economic Reform and Macroeconomic Management, by Mario Blejer, David Burton, Steven Dunaway, and Gyorgy Szapary. 1991.

75. German Unification: Economic Issues, edited by Leslie Lipschitz and Donogh McDonald. 1990.

74. The Impact of the European Community's Internal Market on the EFTA, by Richard K. Abrams, Peter K. Cornelius, Per L. Hedfors, and Gunnar Tersman. 1990.

73. The European Monetary System: Developments and Perspectives, by Horst Ungerer, Jouko J. Hauvonen, Augusto Lopez-Claros, and Thomas Mayer. 1990.

72. The Czech and Slovak Federal Republic: An Economy in Transition, by Jim Prust and an IMF Staff Team. 1990.

71. MULTIMOD Mark II: A Revised and Extended Model, by Paul Masson, Steven Symansky, and Guy Meredith. 1990.

70. The Conduct of Monetary Policy in the Major Industrial Countries: Instruments and Operating Procedures, by Dallas S. Batten, Michael P. Blackwell, In-Su Kim, Simon E. Nocera, and Yuzuru Ozeki. 1990.

69. International Comparisons of Government Expenditure Revisited: The Developing Countries, 1975–86, by Peter S. Heller and Jack Diamond. 1990.

68. Debt Reduction and Economic Activity, by Michael P. Dooley, David Folkerts-Landau, Richard D. Haas, Steven A. Symansky, and Ralph W. Tryon. 1990.

67. The Role of National Saving in the World Economy: Recent Trends and Prospects, by Bijan B. Aghevli, James M. Boughton, Peter J. Montiel, Delano Villanueva, and Geoffrey Woglom. 1990.

66. The European Monetary System in the Context of the Integration of European Financial Markets, by David Folkerts-Landau and Donald J. Mathieson. 1989.

65. Managing Financial Risks in Indebted Developing Countries, by Donald J. Mathieson, David Folkerts-Landau, Timothy Lane, and Iqbal Zaidi. 1989.

64. The Federal Republic of Germany: Adjustment in a Surplus Country, by Leslie Lipschitz, Jeroen Kremers, Thomas Mayer, and Donogh McDonald. 1989.

63. Issues and Developments in International Trade Policy, by Margaret Kelly, Naheed Kirmani, Miranda Xafa, Clemens Boonekamp, and Peter Winglee. 1988.

62. The Common Agricultural Policy of the European Community: Principles and Consequences, by Julius Rosenblatt, Thomas Mayer, Kasper Bartholdy, Dimitrios Demekas, Sanjeev Gupta, and Leslie Lipschitz. 1988.

61. Policy Coordination in the European Monetary System. Part I: The European Monetary System: A Balance Between Rules and Discretion, by Manuel Guitián. Part II: Monetary Coordination Within the European Monetary System: Is There a Rule? by Massimo Russo and Giuseppe Tullio. 1988.

60. Policies for Developing Forward Foreign Exchange Markets, by Peter J. Quirk, Graham Hacche, Viktor Schoofs, and Lothar Weniger. 1988.

59. Measurement of Fiscal Impact: Methodological Issues, edited by Mario I. Blejer and Ke-Young Chu. 1988.

58. The Implications of Fund-Supported Adjustment Programs for Poverty: Experiences in Selected Countries, by Peter S. Heller, A. Lans Bovenberg, Thanos Catsambas, Ke-Young Chu, and Parthasarathi Shome. 1988.

57. The Search for Efficiency in the Adjustment Process: Spain in the 1980s, by Augusto Lopez-Claros. 1988.

56. Privatization and Public Enterprises, by Richard Hemming and Ali M. Mansoor. 1988.

55. Theoretical Aspects of the Design of Fund-Supported Adjustment Programs: A Study by the Research Department of the International Monetary Fund. 1987.

54. Protection and Liberalization: A Review of Analytical Issues, by W. Max Corden. 1987.

53. Floating Exchange Rates in Developing Countries: Experience with Auction and Interbank Markets, by Peter J. Quirk, Benedicte Vibe Christensen, Kyung-Mo Huh, and Toshihiko Sasaki. 1987.

52. Structural Reform, Stabilization, and Growth in Turkey, by George Kopits. 1987.

51. The Role of the SDR in the International Monetary System: Studies by the Research and Treasurer's Departments of the International Monetary Fund. 1987.

50. Strengthening the International Monetary System: Exchange Rates, Surveillance, and Objective Indicators, by Andrew Crockett and Morris Goldstein. 1987.

49. Islamic Banking, by Zubair Iqbal and Abbas Mirakhor. 1987.

48. The European Monetary System: Recent Developments, by Horst Ungerer, Owen Evans, Thomas Mayer, and Philip Young. 1986.

47. Aging and Social Expenditure in the Major Industrial Countries, 1980–2025, by Peter S. Heller, Richard Hemming, Peter W. Kohnert, and a Staff Team from the Fiscal Affairs Department. 1986.

46. Fund-Supported Programs, Fiscal Policy, and Income Distribution: A Study by the Fiscal Affairs Department of the International Monetary Fund. 1986.

45. Switzerland's Role as an International Financial Center, by Benedicte Vibe Christensen. 1986.

44. A Review of the Fiscal Impulse Measure, by Peter S. Heller, Richard D. Haas, and Ahsan H. Mansur. 1986.

42. Global Effects of Fund-Supported Adjustment Programs, by Morris Goldstein. 1986.

41. Fund-Supported Adjustment Programs and Economic Growth, by Mohsin S. Kahn and Malcolm D. Knight. 1985.

39. A Case of Successful Adjustment: Korea's Experience During 1980–84, by Bijan B. Aghevli and Jorge Márquez-Ruarte. 1985.

38. Trade Policy Issues and Developments, by Shailendra J. Anjaria, Naheed Kirmani, and Arne B. Petersen. 1985.

Note: For information on the title and availability of Occasional Papers not listed, please consult the IMF *Publications Catalog* or contact IMF Publication Services. Occasional Paper Nos. 5–26 are $5.00 a copy (academic rate: $3.00); Nos. 27–64 are $7.50 a copy (academic rate: $4.50); and from No. 65 on, the price is $10.00 a copy (academic rate: $7.50).